W0232811

100 Ideas for Primary Teachers:

Wellbeing

Jennifer Murray

BLOOMSBURY EDUCATION

LONDON   OXFORD   NEW YORK   NEW DELHI   SYDNEY

BLOOMSBURY EDUCATION
Bloomsbury Publishing Plc
50 Bedford Square, London, WC1B 3DP, UK
29 Earlsfort Terrace, Dublin 2, Ireland

BLOOMSBURY, BLOOMSBURY EDUCATION and the Diana logo are
trademarks of Bloomsbury Publishing Plc

First published in Great Britain 2024 by Bloomsbury Publishing Ltd

This edition published in Great Britiain 2024 by Bloomsbury Publishing Ltd

Text copyright © Jennifer Murray 2024

Jennifer Murray has asserted her right under the Copyright, Designs and
Patents Act, 1988, to be identified as Author of this work

Bloomsbury Publishing Plc does not have any control over, or responsibility
for, any third-party websites referred to or in this book. All internet addresses
given in this book were correct at the time of going to press. The author and
publisher regret any inconvenience caused if addresses have changed or sites
have ceased to exist, but can accept no responsibility for any such changes

All rights reserved. No part of this publication may be reproduced or
transmitted in any form or by any means, electronic or mechanical, including
photocopying, recording, or any information storage or retrieval system,
without prior permission in writing from the publishers

A catalogue record for this book is available from the British Library

ISBN: PB: 978-1-8019-9369-2; ePDF: 978-1-8019-9368-5;
ePub: 978-1-8019-9370-8

2 4 6 8 10 9 7 5 3 1 (paperback)

Typeset by Newgen KnowledgeWorks Pvt. Ltd., Chennai, India
Printed and bound in India by Replika Press Pvt. Ltd

To find out more about our authors and books visit www.bloomsbury.com
and sign up for our newsletters.

Contents

Acknowledgements

Thank you to Joanna Ramsay at Bloomsbury for her patience, understanding and enthusiasm and for taking a chance on me and my ideas. Thanks also to Cathy Lear for her attention to detail and thought-provoking questions.

Thank you to my family and friends who know what they and this passion project mean to me and who keep me in check around my own wellbeing. Particular gratitude to my Mum: the ultimate 'critical friend' who knows exactly when and how to point out a rogue comma!

Thank you to colleagues, trainees and pupils past and present who have welcomed me and my 'wellbeing hat' into classrooms and lecture spaces. I continue to learn so much from you all.

Finally, as promised, I dedicate this book to Carole, my first TA and very dear friend, who taught me to preserve the magic in classrooms and that wellbeing must always come first. I will keep writing in her memory.

Foreword

One of my favourite wellbeing experts is a psychology professor called Tal Ben Shahar. He was asked what it is that makes the biggest difference to people's wellbeing and he simply answered, 'It's small things, consistently applied'. In other words, it's the small things we weave into our routines and daily habits that build up to make a big difference to how we feel. And that's what I love about this book – it is filled to the brim with small, practical ideas which busy teachers can try out, experiment with and weave into their everyday teaching practices.

Rightly so, Jennifer starts this book with a focus on teacher wellbeing. It's good for teachers to walk the walk and model to their pupils what taking good care of themselves looks like. Teachers are significant role models in children's lives, so a well-rested teacher who actively prioritises their own wellbeing is setting their class a great example to follow. It also makes any teaching of wellbeing skills a lot more authentic.

Which brings me on to the main focus of this book – the practical tools and skills we can teach to children to help improve their wellbeing. There are so many interesting and varied ideas for teachers to try out and I'm confident they will appeal to all children in our rich and diverse classrooms. There are tools to help children recognise and regulate their emotions, and others that aim to get them moving their bodies and increasing physical activity in ways that don't feel like exercise!

We know that teachers have a big impact on children's wellbeing just by being good teachers. But with this book and its fabulous ideas in your toolkit, you'll be able to enhance the impact you have and positively influence children's wellbeing for many years to come.

Adrian Bethune

Introduction

During my final teaching practice, I was warned by a university tutor whom I respect hugely, that if I didn't learn to prioritise my own wellbeing, I'd risk not becoming the teacher I wanted to be. These direct and honest words so early in my career gave a powerful message and have shaped me as an educator. The wellbeing of children, colleagues and trainees has remained a priority for me ever since. I don't claim always to have the balance right for my own wellbeing nor do I have all the answers for others but I can say confidently that every day I have at least one conversation about wellbeing. By way of introduction to the book, I offer you four of my strongest beliefs about wellbeing in education.

Wellbeing as a focus is not new. Long before the COVID-19 pandemic, many schools around the world were already working hard to promote and protect the wellbeing of children. As we begin to understand the impact of lockdowns, social isolation and changes in ways we live and learn, the urgent need to embed effective strategies for wellbeing in educational environments has only increased. The ideas in this book can support educators who are working in settings where wellbeing is already established as a priority. It can also serve as a starting point for anyone in education who knows they want to do more.

Understanding wellbeing is not easy. Whether we're trying to define it in our school policies or trying to decide which part of it to prioritise, wellbeing is a huge, often unwieldy topic. I often say to my trainees at university that I believe teaching is at once the most important and hardest job. I have seen so many educators battle courageously to balance curriculum demands with prioritising children's wellbeing needs and it seems obvious that they need time and resources to do this well. The responsibility is immense and so too should be the support for those who shoulder it in schools.

Approaches to supporting wellbeing should be proactive, responsive, diverse and personalised. The complexity of intersecting challenges faced by humans and the potential impact on wellbeing make it impossible to provide a 'how to' guide to promoting and protecting wellbeing in primary classrooms. My hope is that teachers, support staff and school leaders will be able to dip into some of the suggestions in the book and pick what might work for their own school community. Each idea can be adapted or adjusted to respond to the needs of individual children. Some are presented as whole school or whole class ideas, whereas others are best used for working with individual children or small groups.

Finally, and perhaps most importantly, I believe wholeheartedly that as educators, we cannot pour from an empty cup. In order to offer our best to the children in our classrooms, we have to prioritise our own wellbeing. In my experience, young learners notice when we don't do this and they thrive when we do. I deliberately begin this collection of ideas with a focus on teacher and support staff wellbeing. However you choose to approach using the rest of the book, I hope you begin by exploring the ideas which focus on your own wellbeing.

How to use this book

This book includes quick, easy and practical ideas for you to dip in and out of to help you promote wellbeing.

Parts 1 and 10 contain ideas to use as a teacher, with colleagues or with the school community; parts 2 - 9 contain ideas to use with children.

Each idea includes:

- a catchy title, easy to refer to and share with your colleagues
- an interesting quote linked to the idea
- a summary of the idea in bold, making it easy to flick through the book and identify an idea you want to use at a glance
- a step-by-step guide to implementing the idea.

Each idea also includes one or more of the following:

Teaching tip

Practical tips and advice for how and how not to run the activity or put the idea into practice.

Taking it further

Ideas and advice for how to extend the idea or develop it further.

Bonus idea ★

There are 46 bonus ideas in this book that are extra-exciting, extra-original and extra-interesting.

Share how you use these ideas and find out what other practitioners have done using **#100ideas**.

Online resources for this book can be found at www.bloomsbury.pub/100-ideas-primary-wellbeing.

Filling your cup first

Part 1

Comfort, stretch, challenge

'Making time for this level of reflection has really helped me to recognise where I'm coping and where I need support.'
Early Career Teacher – London, UK

Most teachers do a lot to help children identify their strengths and areas for development in learning. Stopping to think about our own comfort, stretch and challenge zones in terms of our roles can be so informative. This simple individual task can be extended to support collaboration among school staff and to promote professional development.

Using a simple graphic (an example is available from the online resources) of three concentric circles, label the centre of the image 'comfort', the middle ring 'stretch' and the outer ring 'challenge'. Before you start, take time to reflect on the diversity of your role. No two days are the same in schools and recognising the demands of our roles as educators is important.

Begin by reflecting on the comfort zone. Which elements of your role feel relatively straightforward? Which parts of your professional practice would colleagues identify as your strengths? This can start as an individual reflective task but may be supported by dialogue with a critical friend or trusted colleague – sometimes help is needed to identify strengths in our day-to-day practice.

Repeat this process with the stretch and challenge sections. The stretch zone is the category where you may need some support or may not be full of confidence but the task still feels manageable. The challenge section should be used for the parts of the role which feel tricky even when support is available.

Taking it further

Around the outside of the concentric circles, consider reflecting honestly on triggers in the workplace. Be clear about how what happens in school may have a negative impact on your wellbeing. If you feel comfortable, sharing some of these triggers in a wider team or with senior leadership can support small adjustments which can have a big impact on wellbeing.

Bonus idea ★

Reviewing the comfort, stretch and challenge zones at the beginning, middle and end of an academic year can be helpful. This can support you to recognise where support has been available to you and, if appropriate, where your professional confidence has increased.

Who's your radiator?

'Taking time as a whole staff to stop and reflect on who can help us to help ourselves in terms of wellbeing was a game changer!'
Wellbeing Lead – Edinburgh, UK

As teachers we know that collaboration can support learning. When we work well together our workload can reduce, we feel more connected and we can benefit from each other's understanding. This simple reflective task allows teachers and other adults in school to work out who is part of their support network.

Introduce the idea of radiators (people who warm you up, support you and help you feel more equipped to promote and protect your own wellbeing) and drains (those who are perhaps quick to share a moan or point out a difficulty in school) in a staff meeting.

As individuals, each teacher or other adult in the school completes the 'Who's your radiator?' reflection task, which involves identifying key people both in and beyond the school community who can support with wellbeing.

The 'Who's your radiator?' prompt sheet (available from the online resources) provides some guiding categories to help facilitate this reflection, including:

- 'Who can I go to if I feel overwhelmed with my workload?'
- 'Who can I go to if I'm worried about dealing with a challenging professional conversation?'
- 'Who can I got to if I need a walk and talk?'
- 'Who can I go to for a coaching conversation?'.

Taking it further

Having a board in a staff area with the title 'I'm looking for...' can be a simple extension for this activity to ensure that lasting collaborative connections are made between staff to support wellbeing. These could include statements such as 'I'm looking for someone who's got a great system for speeding up their marking' or 'I'm looking for someone who could share ideas for discussing bullying with parents/carers'.

Bonus idea ★

Consider completing a positive snowstorm (Idea 37) as a staff and encourage colleagues to get comfortable with sharing and receiving compliments!

Make time to take time

'Looking at my calendar in a different way has helped to make self-care a priority. Small adjustments have felt like they've helped to chip away and shift feelings of overwhelm. The impact on my energy and my happiness at work has been significant.'
School-based Trainee Teacher – London, UK

Teachers are busy and to-do lists often feel endless. These simple ideas for protecting your downtime can help to make sure that you're energised, rested and ready to be the best teacher you can be.

Taking it further

Consider how diarising downtime can help to maintain this structure. Simply writing in your calendar or diary what your non-school-related activities are will help to keep them at the forefront of your mind and as high on the priority list as possible. Using ideas from the ways to wellbeing reviews (**Idea 21**) can help with identifying the sorts of activities which can be plotted in your protected calendar time.

Consider how much autonomy you have over your timetable and, where possible, make adjustments to the lessons you teach to ensure you avoid an influx of marking all at once. If you know you're going to have 30 books to mark for one of your lessons, try to do some on-the-spot marking for other lessons or weave in some peer assessment to avoid an overload on one day.

Identify your protected days, when finishing work in time for some rest and relaxation is non-negotiable. Be realistic about how often this will be possible and try to form a habit of always protecting that time. Consider using the sunshine file (**Idea 7**) to log any of these protected times which you notice as being particularly positive or impactful.

Front and centre stage

'This helps us to remember that the focus of our role is being here for the children. They are our priority.'
Year 2 Teacher – Buckinghamshire, UK

When things get busy in school and huge demands are placed on teachers' time, one of the hardest things is to prioritise. Most of us have experienced the week-to-week rollover of items on our to-do lists. Lists of tasks help us to stay organised, which fuels a sense of control and so improves our wellbeing. This idea can help when overwhelm creeps in.

A happy, healthy, well-rested teacher is, surely, the best resource in a classroom, so it's vital to protect teachers from being overwhelmed by unnecessary tasks. To-do lists can be a great way to organise things to be done in your classroom or admin to be completed throughout the week. Asking yourself two key questions can help to identify the most important tasks and separate the 'need to do' from the 'nice to do'. Firstly, consider the priority people – the children. When faced with another addition to the list, and when reviewing your priority tasks at the end of the day, ask yourself 'If I postpone this, will the children's learning suffer tomorrow?'. It should only move to the top of your list if the answer is yes. Next, consider yourself as the key resource in the classroom and ask 'Will it positively impact my wellbeing if I complete the task now?'. If the impact of task completion isn't going to be significant on your wellbeing or children's learning, then it can wait.

Keeping key people (the learners and yourself as teacher) front and centre stage when making decisions about workload can help you to manage overwhelm.

Taking it further

It's important to acknowledge that often the jobs which land on teachers' lists are set by others. I have worked with colleagues who have kept track of their to-do lists, complete with a 'front and centre stage' section every day. They found this a helpful foundation for conversations with school leaders about managing workload. Sometimes, it can be helpful for us (and those who delegate to us!) to see exactly what we're prioritising on a day-to-day basis; often open conversations about priorities can lead to support being offered or adjustments made.

No can be a full sentence

'This helps us to remember that every colleague has a life beyond school and that this should be respected. A genuine understanding of boundaries should be part of regular staff conversation.'
Special Educational Needs Coordinator – Oxfordshire, UK

Most teachers I've worked with have been quick to offer support to colleagues, picking up an extra break duty or lending a hand with a display, for example. While this proactive, 'can do' attitude might be the very behaviour which promotes wellbeing for colleagues, it could set a risky precedent.

Setting boundaries at work can lead to a healthier work-life balance and can have a huge impact on teacher wellbeing. Some of the best suggestions I've observed form this idea. Firstly, remember that 'No' can constitute a full sentence. Understanding when it's ok to say 'no' at work can be difficult; knowing your own boundaries is a good starting point. Questions to ask yourself before answering a request include (but are definitely not limited to!), 'Is there a realistic timeframe?', 'Is this job actually under my remit?' and 'Am I the person to complete this task in the most productive and time-efficient way?'. If the answers are 'no', then the answer to the request could be too! Obviously, using 'no' as a full sentence isn't always realistic so it can help to practise language focussed on compromise, for example, 'I understand why you're asking for my help but I'd need something taken from my workload to have capacity.' or 'I'd love to support you but I can't make time this week, would it work to help later?'. Initial attempts at establishing and upholding boundaries in the workplace can be uncomfortable but also hugely impactful. A less intimidating way to exercise professional boundaries is to use your calendar to block off time specifically for your own preparation and planning.

> **Bonus idea** ★
>
> Time after school can be a productive opportunity to focus on jobs within your own classroom. This time is precious but is often derailed by well-intentioned visiting colleagues. Consider setting up an agreement in a staff meeting that those who want to work without disruption can do so in their classrooms with the door closed as a signal. Those willing to discuss ideas or chat to colleagues can opt for a literal open-door policy.

You are what you eat (and drink!)

'Applying my teacher planner skills to nutrition and hydration is a simple act of self-care that helped me to notice patterns and increase my energy before, during and after work.'
Year 3 Early Career Teacher – London, UK

Teachers are great planners. They plan lessons, adaptations to lessons, assessments, adaptations to assessments... the list goes on! With a pressured workload, nutrition and hydration can slip down the list. A weekly planner can help to prioritise fuelling yourself for everything a school day brings.

This can be an individual activity or may also prove particularly supportive (and sustainable) when completed with a colleague. This isn't designed to be nutritional advice but rather an easy format through which to reflect on your patterns and build healthy habits which work for you. Begin by tracking your energy levels over the course of a week. In a diary or online calendar, colour code the beginning, middle and end of your working day in red (low energy – feeling really tired), amber (sufficient energy but could have more), green (full of energy). Notice where your energy dips are and think about how this might relate to your fuel!

Using a simple weekly planner (available from the online resources), organise your meal plans as much as you can to ensure a healthy, consistent fuel plan for your working week. Remember to factor in high energy snacks to help your physical wellbeing for those after school tasks.

Taking it further

Take the hydration part of your weekly plan into the classroom and engage learners in also developing an awareness of how good hydration habits can support their wellbeing. Creating a fuelling commitment (where children choose one healthy habit they're going to adopt and log it for a week) is a great way to make this a collaborative, community practice.

Bonus idea ★

Making and sustaining one simple change per month can help form powerful wellbeing habits. This could be something as simple as refilling your water bottle once more than normal every day (and emptying it!) or always having some fruit after school.

The sunshine file

'My 'sunshine file' is my diary. Each time I remember, I draw a little sun and write something down which made me smile. Sometimes it's a positive interaction or a student having a 'lightbulb' moment. This means when I look back, I remember the moments of joy which might otherwise be forgotten in the busy-ness of my job.'
Lecturer in Primary Education – London, UK

The sunshine file helps educators to develop the habit of recording and referring back to moments of joy. The focus of this activity is building habits into daily practice which recognise the positives in our professional experiences.

Taking it further

Try sharing this idea with your class. A great way to promote children's awareness of positive moments in their learning is to model this explicitly. Once you have become used to spotting sunshine moments, perhaps display these on your board or tell your class about them when you're doing the register.

The sunshine file involves a commitment to noticing positive moments (however small!) in a school day and aiming to log at least one a day. It's really important to make sure they're logged as it's easy to forget the positive moments whilst juggling the challenges of the role. This could be done in lots of different ways, is quick and easy and absolutely should not increase workload. For some teachers, simply creating an additional folder in your email inbox where you can file positives can be a sunshine file, although this tends to be more a space where *ad hoc* 'good news' is filed away. Revisiting positive emails from parents, carers or colleagues can be a great strategy to break through a cloud but the sunshine file takes this one step further by creating healthy habits.

Decide where you'll store your sunshine moments and when you'll add them to your file. Picking a set daily time to reflect on your sunshine moment (while travelling home, washing the dishes, writing the date on your board for the following day in school) can help to sustain the habit of noticing the day's sunshine. Write a few words or draw a doodle of the moment of sunshine you noticed. This can be as simple as every child responding to a behaviour expectation you set in your classroom. It could involve observations you make of an individual child grasping a tricky concept in a lesson or it might be a reflection on a really helpful supportive interaction you have had with a colleague in school. However big or small, keeping a sunshine file is about cultivating the habit of noticing the good.

It is important to make sure you look back at the moments of sunshine you recorded. Some people might find this beneficial to do once every half term. It can be fun to do this in a group with trusted colleagues, as sharing sunshine moments can inspire others to see the positives in their working environments. Your sunshine file may also become a resource to reach for when work is tough or morale is low. Reminding yourself that challenges aren't constant by reflecting on examples of positive times can be a really motivating and reassuring activity.

Don't forget to share the sunshine! If you find the practice helpful, let others know. If the idea of a sunshine file catches on in your year group or key stage, try adding a sunshine share to the team meeting agenda. It can bring some light to a long list of updates or administrative tasks.

> **Bonus idea** ★
>
> At the end of an academic year, sharing extracts of sunshine with a whole staff group can be a positive reflection activity. At your final whole staff meeting, teachers and support staff could add anonymous sunshine moments to a box or online pinboard and these could be read out to the team. Some colleagues might have positive memories sparked by listening to sunshine moments.

Bring, brag and borrow

'This changed the way our staff meetings were structured. It took a while for people to be comfortable with it but, on the whole, we're much more open about our strengths as a staff now.'
Assistant Headteacher – Oxfordshire, UK

When things get busy in schools, it can sometimes feel tricky to share best practice or learn from colleagues. Connection and collaboration can support teacher wellbeing and this simple agenda item can promote culture change over time.

Introduce the idea of the 3Bs in a staff meeting, early in the term. Collaboratively decide on a structure which fits with the size of the school and the number of teachers and support staff who are attending meetings. Add 'Bring, brag and borrow' to the staff meeting agenda and allocate a five-minute slot for sharing best practice with the whole staff. Over the course of the academic year, a different teacher or year group team should be responsible for the 'bring and brag' in each whole staff meeting. Other colleagues should be encouraged to borrow an idea and, where possible, a staffroom board can be used to record ideas and share feedback from borrowers.

It might be helpful to focus the bring and brag on ideas, strategies or approaches which help to promote and protect wellbeing. This could include a time-saving tip for marking, a collaborative approach to planning or something else which has allowed professionals to thrive in their setting. Alternatively, senior leadership may wish to widen the focus to use bring and brag as an opportunity to create a culture of pride in professional practice. Celebrating good practice and asking colleagues to self-identify strengths can be transformative in terms of staff self-esteem.

Taking it further

Give each staff member a metal keyring and each time someone presents a 'bring, brag and borrow idea', ask them to come with a small, laminated summary for each colleague. Staff can then add their card to their own keyring to build up and refer back to a collection of innovative ideas.

A cup of kindness

'When I found the cup of kindness on my desk on a dreary October morning, I realised that small gestures can make a huge impact on how teachers feel. The treats were so gratefully received and made me determined to spread the kindness and pass it on.'
Teacher in Second Class – Dublin, Ireland

The cup of kindness is a simple whole staff initiative which involves surprising a colleague with a mug full of treats to boost their wellbeing. It relies on everyone participating over the course of a term or academic year (depending on staff numbers) so is best introduced at a staff meeting.

You'll need one or two special mugs for this initiative. The more distinctive they are, the less likely they are to get lost in the staffroom cupboard! Introduce the idea of the cup of kindness and brainstorm the sorts of things staff might be excited to receive. Suggestions include chocolate, tea bags, a new piece of stationery, a break duty cover voucher; these could be recorded somewhere for staff to look back at for inspiration. Choose a day that the cup of kindness should be left anonymously and a place where names of those who receive the cup can be recorded. This ensures that all staff get a cup of kindness surprise at least once a year and is best stored in the staffroom so that people can check who's already had one before they pass it on! Start with two people secretly filling the cups of kindness and leaving them for the first lucky colleagues to discover on the agreed day.

Taking it further

This idea can be developed into a more sustained system of secret surprises if staff morale is boosted by the cup of kindness. Try developing an optional secret pal system where, at the start of the year, interested staff fill out a short survey about their favourite treats/hobbies/ interests. The secret pal coordinator then collects all the surveys and gives them out (at random) to participating staff. Secret pals then leave a treat on their allocated colleague's desk once a term and on their birthday.

Stop, start, continue

'This idea really needs Senior Leadership Team support behind it. In order to impact change, there has to be a culture of open communication and all staff need to have a voice.'
Year 2 Teacher – Buckinghamshire, UK

All schools are different in terms of expectations for planning, assessing, marking and reporting. Lots of teachers identify these as core areas which, depending on expectations, can impact workload and wellbeing in significant ways. Collating feedback for senior leaders using this simple structure can promote teacher-voice and autonomy in decision making about workload management.

Taking it further

Once the stop, start, continue approach has become familiar to all staff, it is useful to revisit requests and suggestions as part of action planning. When reviewing targets set for whole school development, consider how closely strategic development priorities align with the staff voice. Empowering staff to feel like they have an impact on ways of working and professional expectations can have a huge impact on wellbeing.

The first thing to consider is how best to gather constructive and honest feedback from hardworking and busy teachers. My experience is that these sorts of conversations are best structured in small groups, ideally a year group or small key stage team where there is a shared understanding and experience of the responsibilities, positives and challenges of a specific role. Ideally, the feedback conversations should be led by someone who can confidently and respectfully encourage everyone's voices. Depending on staff morale and the extent to which wellbeing work is seen as meaningful, discussions may become quite emotive and it can be helpful to establish some ground rules and a shared aim from the outset.

Begin by putting three large pieces of paper on different tables and label them 'stop', 'start' or 'continue'. Introduce the thought-sharing opportunity as a constructive attempt to identify themes about workload challenges and the impact on wellbeing. The 'stop' piece of paper is where issues can be noted. Staff should consider what their core concerns are; what they're being asked to do which is negatively impacting wellbeing.

In contrast to the issues raised on the 'stop' sheet, the 'continue' sheet should become a list of what is already going well in the school and should therefore be maintained in order to protect staff wellbeing. Again, multiple perspectives are key here. Consider how support staff can be represented in the discussions and how their wellbeing needs might align with or differ from the needs of a class teacher. Finally, the 'start' sheet is a space for creative, innovative ideas to be proposed by the staff group. It is essential that there's a safe and professional climate for this sort of conversation. Where possible, encourage colleagues to initial their contributions; this not only shows whether the perspective is a shared view but also allows for further dialogue about potentially culture-changing ideas.

What's really important with this idea is that the information goes somewhere. Ideally, Senior Leaders should assign the task to the whole staff and then report back with a 'you said, we did' response to show that pinch points, workload challenges and creative suggestions have been acknowledged and acted on.

Bonus idea ★

A simple three-word survey for staff might be a helpful precursor to this activity. Asking colleagues to state anonymously the top three workload challenges which impact their wellbeing will allow you to identify the themes for the stop, start, continue activity.

Leading with language

Part 2

A working word wall for feelings

'Using a word wall enabled my 1:1 to express his feelings in a safe and creative way. It became his voice for his emotions, significantly reduced his angry physical outbursts and equipped him with another way to share his feelings.'
Learning Support Assistant – Surrey, UK

By creating a working word wall to help children articulate their emotions, teachers not only support the development of emotional intelligence but also show that being able to express feelings is a priority! Ideally, this working wall should be accessible to children and visitors to the classroom so that it can be updated and used regularly.

Teaching tip

Display the feelings words and associated images on the working wall and encourage children to add to the wall when they identify a particular feeling in themselves or a peer. Model adding to the wall as a class teacher too.

Taking it further

The working word wall for feelings can be used in lessons; encourage children to choose emotions from the wall to describe characters or use the wall as the basis for a drama lessons. The more connections made to the wall, the higher on the agenda emotional articulation will stay.

In a circle discussion with your class, show pictures of children and adults' faces and ask the children to reflect on the emotions they think might be being shown. Encourage children to use different words to express the feelings they observe and record the range of feelings words they identify.

If you already use working walls in your classroom, the children will be aware that they are a resource to be updated and adapted by everyone in the learning community. Discuss why having a working word wall for feelings might help promote wellbeing in the classroom. Encourage the children to think about the impact on their wellbeing of being able to express their feelings and the way they build relationships with each other.

Partner the children and ask them to design a word card including a feelings word from the list and a drawing of how this feeling might look for them or a peer.

Mirror, mirror, on the wall

'Children as young as three beginning to label their emotions and understand the feelings of their peers was transformational for our classroom.'
Foundation Stage Teacher – Dubai, UAE

Building time into a busy learning day to focus on emotional wellbeing can be tricky. However, giving children the chance to reflect on, identify and communicate their feelings with trusted adults can be the catalyst for a healthy learning environment. This simple activity doubles as a self-registration and self-regulation opportunity. It can be particularly powerful for younger children or those who may struggle to verbalise their feelings.

If you can, fix a mirror to the wall at a child-friendly height. Alternatively, cover a space on the wall with reflective paper. What's important is that it's at a height at which all the children in the class can see themselves. Next, around the outside of the mirror, display a range of emotion cards (faces showing an emotion with the corresponding word) including an 'other' in case the choices don't fit for your class on any given day.

Introduce the self-registration system to your class. Each child gets a 'mini-me' or their name on a laminated card, which they must find in the box as they arrive in the morning. They then have a good look in the mirror (ideally with a friend) to identify how they appear to be feeling. Using the cue cards to help, the child then sticks their name next to the most appropriate feelings card as a way of self-registering and reflecting on their emotions at the start of the day. Some younger children will benefit from trying this task using puppets or toys to begin with. They can be asked to identify emotions each puppet or toy might be displaying or alternatively, use the puppet to act out and communicate a particular emotion with a friend.

> **Bonus idea** ★
>
> If you have additional adults in your classroom, ask them to oversee the mirror registration to facilitate targeted conversations if they are needed. As the children become used to identifying their own emotions (and how facial expressions/ body language might communicate these), the activity could be extended to allow children to reflect throughout their day and move their name to a new feelings card if appropriate. This is a great way to demonstrate to young children that feelings change!

17

Fine, thanks. No, thanks.

'Before introducing this to my class, I noticed how often I gave an automatic response when someone asked how I was. Introducing the importance of honesty about our wellbeing has taken time but has paid off and made our classroom a kinder place to learn!'
Year 5 Teacher – London, UK

Schools are, without doubt, busy places to work and learn. While we know it is important to create a sense of belonging for learners and teachers alike, it can be hard to make the time to check in on those around us. This is a simple activity to remind everyone in the school community how valuable it is to listen actively and respond honestly to the question 'How are you?'.

Teaching tip

Take time to explain to the children that sometimes people won't always feel comfortable opening up about how they're feeling. Reinforce that this is OK too and that, as individuals, we always have choices about how or when we express our feelings.

Taking it further

You could combine this idea with register affirmations (**Idea 56**) – and ask children to respond to their names at register time with an honest response to the question 'How are you?'. This activity is best saved for later in the academic year when a safe, supportive and wellbeing-focussed learning environment has been established so that everyone can contribute comfortably.

Begin by observing how often people respond with 'Fine, thanks!' when asked how they are. You could keep tally over the course of a day or a week and then share with the children what you noticed. Depending on the age of the children, you could then set them the secret mission of asking as many adults and/or children how they are during break/lunchtimes and challenge them to keep a tally of how many people respond with 'Fine, thanks!' instead of anything more detailed. Older, more independent learners could turn this into a data collection task where they survey people in their school community and analyse their answers.

Discuss with the children how, sometimes, a genuine response to the question 'How are you?' can be 'Fine, thanks' but that, no matter what age we are, we can use language to model being honest and open about how we are really. Build up a word bank of responses to use instead of 'Fine, thanks', and encourage the children to notice when peers or other adults open up about their feelings.

What's in your backpack?

'Having something tangible helps to reinforce the idea that wellbeing can be linked to every area of life. If this is grasped by the children, conversations about wellbeing will flow naturally and effectively throughout the school community.'
Primary Drama Specialist – London, UK

Promoting and protecting wellbeing in primary classrooms goes beyond teachers telling children what to do when something goes wrong. Empowering children and young people to identify proactive and responsive ways to support their wellbeing can help learners to be independent and to support each other. This practical wellbeing backpack idea brings the strategies to life.

Begin by introducing your own backpack to the children and discuss the importance of using times when we have positive wellbeing, to focus on what to do when we don't. This is a great opportunity to be explicit about the language of wellbeing used in your classroom. For example, everyone has mental and physical health; sometimes it's positive, sometimes it's challenging. Inside your backpack put some tangible objects that, depending on the age of the children, you can show, or they can pick out of the backpack. Encourage the children to guess how each item might relate to your wellbeing and be as creative as you can be. Some objects you might consider putting in your backpack if they are relevant: water for hydration, a book for switching off, some sports kit if you use being active as a way to positive wellbeing, something which reminds you of someone important in your life, a photograph of a place which brings you calm, some healthy food or a phone (either for connecting with others or for playing music you like).

> **Bonus idea** ★
>
> Follow up your sharing with a planning task for the children to complete in small groups or pairs. Ask them to think about what they would put in their wellbeing backpack and why. Creating a luggage tag postcard, a mini backpack frame for inside a school diary or a display of drawings/collages about what goes in their wellbeing backpacks can help to remind learners of all the resources they have to hand to promote and protect their wellbeing.

What if?

'So many of my pupils refer back to their 'What if' display when particular emotions arise. I can step back and observe their self-regulation.'
Head of Infants – London, UK

This whole class task challenges children to support each other with self-regulation. It builds on other ideas in the book which promote the identification of feelings (for example Ideas 12 and 13). Through this simple activity, learners are encouraged to respond resourcefully to a range of wellbeing indicators.

Firstly, try 'Fine, thanks. No, thanks.' (**Idea 13**) as a starter activity and note down the different responses given by the children/adults in your classroom. If possible, group themes of responses (for example tired, exhausted, weary; and nervous, worried, anxious) and allocate one or two themes to each table group with the prompt 'What if I am... .' (For example 'What if I am lonely?') With adult support if necessary, ask the children to come up with as many ways as possible to respond to their wellbeing indicator. Children could draw or write their responses. (For example, 'If I'm lonely, I can visit a friendship stop in the playground or I can ask a grown up for help.') Encouraging creativity (but also realism!) is important and this can be directed through mini-plenaries to pause and sense-check the ideas which are being documented on the table.

Collate the key responses to each 'What if?' prompt and ask children to choose one they would like to design a display card about. Giving children this responsibility for a response can be empowering and allows a sense of shared ownership of the strategy.

Taking it further

Some classes will benefit from greater structure for this idea to work well. It may be helpful to split the thought-sharing paper into three and ask children to think about the ways they could respond at home, in the classroom and in the wider school community. This can encourage a more diverse response to the 'What if?' prompt and support the inclusion of all learners.

Compliments chain

'This is such a simple idea and it really helped to shape the culture of kindness I wanted in my classroom.'
Year 4 Teacher – London, UK

Teaching children explicitly about kindness and supporting a sense of belonging in a classroom can be powerful. This simple tangible idea can be used with any age group and just requires some paperclips for your classroom to become a compliment zone.

In a circle discussion, share some paperclips with the children but don't tell them what they're for initially. Ask them to decide with a partner what it means to give someone a compliment.

Share examples of when they've given or received a compliment. If your class are able to, it can be helpful to ask them to think about diversifying their compliments so that they don't all focus on physical appearance. Model some ideas of how you might compliment a or colleague by focussing on non-physical traits, for example: 'I really like how patient you are with helping us in our learning' or 'You make everyone feel welcome'. Or pre-plan a compliment for every child in the class; read each one out and get the children to guess who it might be for. This can be a lovely opportunity for children to notice the good in each other and often leads to lots of smiles in a classroom! Once the purpose, meaning and content of compliments have been explored, introduce the compliments chain challenge.

Explain to the children that each time you or any other adults in the classroom notice a compliment being shared, a paperclip will be added to the chain. The aim is to hang the chain of paperclips from the top of the whiteboard edge and extend it to reach the floor by the end of the month/term.

> **Teaching tip**
>
> Depending on your school's policy, you could set a reward as an incentive for the chain to grow but for most children, the giving and receiving of compliments becomes an incentive in itself!

Great wall of gratitude

'Our classroom became a happier place to learn as children noticed they had lots to be grateful for! I also found myself noticing when I needed to be a bit more positive in the language I was using. Gratitude practices have been really powerful in my personal wellbeing work and it has been lovely to bring them into my classroom too.'
Year 2 Teacher – Dubai, UAE

Focussing on wins, no matter how small, can help learners develop a sustainable resilient outlook towards learning and life. This simple strategy can work with just an accessible wall display, some sticky notes and some teacher-modelling.

Taking it further

Some children may benefit from the chance to keep a personal gratitude journal. This could include images or writing and could be shared with a trusted adult as an individual approach to developing gratitude and a positive attitude.

Create a great wall of gratitude space on a display board or spare wall area – a quieter part of your classroom might be useful to promote contemplation. You might want to get creative and use brick shapes to make a realistic-looking wall, but this isn't essential. A blank piece of paper with the heading 'Great wall of gratitude' will do! Introduce the idea of gratitude in an age-appropriate way. Some ideas could include: a lesson on people who are special to us in Reception; a class discussion on things we know we're lucky to have in Key Stage 1; or a reflective task about the opportunities we've had so far in school as part of Key Stage 2 transition.

Model how noticing small things can help us feel happier. You could link this to promoting positive behaviour by framing your praise with 'I am grateful that...' stems. Another great way to start getting children used to noticing things they're grateful for is to model this really explicitly by keeping a list on your whiteboard of all the things you notice with gratitude in one day. These might be personal, for example a strong coffee before your class arrives, a smooth journey to school or having your favourite lunch! They could also be classroom-focussed such as noticing children showing determination in learning or helping each other to succeed. What's important at the earliest stages of trying this idea is that the children recognise that there are endless opportunities to be grateful, we'll all be grateful for different things and there are no wrong answers when the question 'What are you grateful for?' is posed.

In a whole class launch lesson, invite all children to identify one thing they're grateful for to start off the display and add these to the wall on sticky notes or brick shapes. Encourage visitors to your class (colleagues, parents, other pupils) to do the same. Children can draw, write or describe what they're grateful for with or without adult support. It can be really powerful for children to observe their trusted adults expressing gratitude so try to involve your colleagues in adding to the great wall of gratitude.

Encourage children to notice the positives in their own time and leave a supply of sticky notes/brick shapes ready for them. Posts can be made anonymously if children choose to, however, many children tend to be keen to express their gratitude and have their own awareness and positivity celebrated by their teachers and peers. Make sure you go back to the wall and encourage children to share what they can see. By the end of the year, it should be a busy wall!

> **Bonus idea** ★
>
> Consider whether having a gratitude assembly might be a good opportunity to share reflections across classes. If more than one class adopts this idea, a whole school assembly could become a very positive celebration and an opportunity to reflect on small wins.

Bubble time

'Bubble time has created moments for children to stop before they pop!'
Drama Teacher and Children's Mental Health Lead – Surrey, UK

We all feel happier when we're being listened to, but classrooms are busy places with lots to accomplish. This simple visual tool gives pupils a voice in promoting and protecting their own wellbeing and helps develop key relationships.

Teaching tip

My experience of using this approach is that sometimes, once bubble time is offered, some of the original feelings may have gone or changed. This is all good learning! This activity can, however, be a great way of identifying children who have persistent challenges with regulating particular emotions.

Taking it further

Discussing with the children that feelings are not 'good' or 'bad' and should just be noticed is an important foundation for supporting self-regulation without judgement. It can be a helpful reminder for adults too!

You will need a hula hoop, bubble wrap, string and a Velcro-backed name card for every child in your class. Wrap the bubble wrap round the hula hoop and hang it somewhere near the teacher's desk or display it at child height on a wall. Introduce the giant bubble to your class.

- Discuss as a group how feelings come and go like bubbles but that sometimes it's important to talk to an adult if help is needed to navigate these feelings.
- Tell children that if they need some 1:1 discussion time with the teacher or another trusted adult about a feeling or worry, they should add their name to the bubble.
- They can then expect the teacher to offer bubble time before the next break or lunchtime; a time in which they can discuss their worry.
- Share ideas as a class about the sorts of feelings/worries/thoughts you'd ask for bubble time for. Children should be clear that if they feel unsafe, they should not wait for a bubble time opportunity.
- Agree as a class how someone will respond to their friends adding their name to the bubble (with kindness and without judgement or intervention).
- Check the bubble before breaks and lunchtimes to ensure that children have an opportunity to voice their feelings.

Wellbeing detectives

'A simple approach to encourage children to understand what wellbeing really means to them!'
Year 2 Teacher – Birmingham, UK

This idea helps to highlight the complexities of wellbeing and the ways in which the physical, mental, social, cognitive and spiritual dimensions of wellbeing are connected. Best used as a whole school approach, this idea provides a fortnightly focus and consolidation opportunity which help embed wellbeing as a priority in school.

In an assembly, launch a dimension of wellbeing every fortnight. Explore children's initial understanding of what the dimension means, how that type of wellbeing can be promoted and protected, and what situations/challenges might put it at risk. Display the dimension somewhere prominent in each classroom and in shared learning spaces (such as the school hall, playground or corridors). During the first week of the fortnight, encourage conversations between teachers and pupils, amongst staff and between children to raise the profile of that dimension. This can be through posing simple register questions, for example, if focussing on cognitive wellbeing children can be asked to respond to the register by answering the question 'What helps you feel ready to learn?'. In the second week of the fortnight, in-class learning can be extended or consolidated by connecting with parents, carers and families. Set the children challenges which are age-appropriate. For example, if the dimension in focus is physical wellbeing, Year 6 pupils could look out for ideas in the community or extra-curricular clubs and then design a physical activity resource or playground circuit, while Year 1 could look out for healthy food choices at home and then design posters for the school cafeteria.

Taking it further

An important part of this idea is that children develop an understanding of how physical, mental, social, cognitive and spiritual wellbeing can be connected.

It's also key that each fortnight concludes with a detectives' celebration where children come together and share all the strategies they've found out about. There are lots of opportunities for cross-curricular learning and cross-phase engagement here. The more teachers and school leaders get involved, the more engaged the children will be.

What do we mean by wellbeing?

'Having a shared understanding of what wellbeing means to us has really helped to establish a new focus. It took time and lengthy discussions to establish a consensus but the work has been completely worth it.'
Deputy Headteacher – London, UK

To get the whole community involved in an initiative, many schools will first ensure a shared understanding of key language. We do this when introducing new policies, approaches to learning and even when identifying school values. Wellbeing work is no different. This idea brings together some tested suggestions for exploring the language of wellbeing and for sharing a school's definition with the wider community.

Teaching tip

Using wellbeing as a basis for collaborative research or non-fiction writing can support older learners to be the experts in their school. Consider opportunities for older children to create short films, flyers or posters to share with younger peers which teach about a school-specific understanding of and vision for wellbeing.

Before any of these ideas can be embedded in practice, staff, children and families need to develop a clear understanding of what wellbeing means in your school's community. From experience, this has worked best when staff are the starting point, with other voices then encouraged to express their views on the staff definitions.

Developing a consensus on what our wellbeing priorities are, how broad our definition is and refining our shared understanding of proactive/reactive strategies to promote and protect wellbeing can be a long-term project. It often reveals a lot about lived values. Once staff have a good understanding of the dimensions of wellbeing and how complex a concept it is, an honest self-audit of priorities is useful.

Begin with asking small groups of staff to focus on a series of questions and to record their responses. It may be more time-efficient to use technology at this stage. Often, basic survey tools can show evidence of themes within responses and support with analysis of feedback. Questions to be discussed and responded to could include:

- 'Which focus within the dimensions of wellbeing gets most coverage within the curriculum?'
- 'Which dimension is the priority in our school just now and why?'
- 'Which dimension of wellbeing is the most under-resourced at the moment?'.

Once these open discussions have happened in staff meetings and feedback has been recorded and analysed, the input with children can begin. Age-appropriate lessons on the different strands under the umbrella term of wellbeing relate well to Personal, Social, Health and Economic education and can be shared with year groups.

In these lessons, it's important to encourage children to become involved in defining each dimension of wellbeing. For example, how do Year 6 understand cognitive wellbeing and how might they then explore this through a buddy discussion with younger learners? Giving children a sense of autonomy and ownership to formulate their definitions in small groups is really important. Where appropriate, contextualise the learning by explaining that the children's input about what each dimension means to them will feed into wider work with teachers, school leaders and parents/carers. Many children will take this role and responsibility very seriously! There could be an opportunity at this stage to involve your school council representatives and encourage some pupil leadership. Perhaps council members could present findings in an assembly or to a focus group of teachers, support staff or parents.

In order to then share the established wellbeing meanings with the wider community, you could start with an established parents' association or set children a homework task to share their learning with parents or carers.

There are opportunities to link these discussions to other ideas in the book including Team tactics (**Idea 93**) or Policy planning (**Idea 95**).

Creating connections

Part 3

Ways to wellbeing reviews

'This helps making wellbeing work really authentic for our children. They're empowered! Getting families involved too has been powerful as children know they have this whole blanket of wellbeing support – home and school aren't separate.'
Year 3 Teacher – Singapore

This is an opportunity to open up dialogue about strategies to promote and protect wellbeing which are accessible and relevant to all. Using this idea supports learners to be independent in managing their own wellbeing needs.

Taking it further

If more than one class develop ways to wellbeing reviews, try extending this collaborative learning opportunity across classes or even key stages.

Begin by leading a class discussion about strategies the children already use to support their wellbeing. Encourage them to think creatively about simple ways that help without requiring many resources. For example, spending time outdoors to help calm themselves or connecting with a trusted adult if something is causing worry. It's important to remember that not all children will have access to wellbeing resources which come at a cost (for example participating in weekend sports events or an art or drama club). Keeping this in mind allows the ways to wellbeing strategy bank to be as inclusive as possible.

Once the children have identified a range of approaches, allocate groups of three children to design a way to wellbeing information sheet for each strategy. Encourage each group of children to first focus on the 'what' by providing a brief explanation of the strategy, approach or idea. They should be reminded to think about an audience who will be reading their ideas for the first time and the importance of making their explanations really clear and descriptive. The next part of the ways to wellbeing review should focus on the 'why'. Here, children should convince. Ideally, the ways to wellbeing information sheets should be visible in the classroom on a working wall so that children can adapt and add to their suggestions when they find new ways of using their strategies to impact wellbeing. They should also be seen as a learning tool for children to engage with independently.

Once the ways to wellbeing have been displayed, encourage children to try out the strategies and add a review when they've used one. This is a great way to encourage collaborative approaches to extending and developing each of the ideas. They can also seek to identify opportunities to use multiple strategies at the same time. If it's more practical, ways to wellbeing reviews could be stored in an accessible folder in the class library and reviews added to them there. The important thing is to make sure children understand that their ideas are being used to support others to protect and promote their wellbeing and that they can learn from one another. This promotes the idea of connections supporting positive wellbeing.

Once the children have completed their ways to wellbeing overviews and reviews have been contributed by their peers, it can be useful to share them with families. Perhaps send a copy of the ways to wellbeing home so that the children can teach their family members or alternatively, build them into an assembly for visitors or display them on a day when parents and carers come to observe learning.

> **Bonus idea** ★
>
> For some children, a personalised approach to this idea can work well. Children could be involved in creating a home/school book of ways to wellbeing which can be shared with parents/carers. This could, if appropriate, be categorised into feelings sections to promote independence and individualised responses to particular experiences of emotional, physical or mental wellbeing.

Send a high five

'Our older children led this initiative and we saw learners across the school actively spotting opportunities to compliment each other!'
Primary 4 Teacher – Lochwinnoch, Scotland

School can be big and sometimes daunting for learners. While teachers work hard to create communities and promote a sense of belonging within their classrooms, whole school approaches to building connections can be trickier. This idea promotes connections across year groups and helps to reinforce expectations for positive, kind and friendly behaviours.

Teaching tip

You can help children by giving them the high five template (available from the online resources) to plan and record their allocated class's high five. The template will help them structure their compliments using prompts on each of the fingertips. Prompts are editable and could include noticing strengths in behaviour, learning approaches or manners for example.

Taking it further

High five awards could be displayed centrally for the whole school or on individual classroom doors.

In individual classes or a whole school assembly, introduce high fives to share compliments or celebrate positive news. Challenge each child to turn to their partner and while counting on their fingers, identify five positive things about them. Once these have been shared, children deliver their high five. This can be an in-class end of day task to encourage positive feedback and encouragement. It's important that teachers begin by discussing how it feels to give and receive high fives. This will encourage a more sustained and engaging whole school initiative.

After learners are accustomed to delivering high fives in their own classrooms, explain that at the start of each week, they will be allocated another class to send a high five to. Throughout the week, encourage your class to keep their nominated class secret but to try and spot them doing great things! This might include being kind in the playground, moving respectfully in corridors or showing positive behaviour choices at lunch. Get the class to record all the things they have observed before choosing two children to deliver the high five to their nominated class at the end of the week. This idea works well when all high fives are delivered at the same time.

My trusted grownup

'This is a key way for children to decide who they build connections with and who can help them feel safe in school.'
Primary 4 Teacher – Lochwinnoch, Scotland

This idea is an example of how closely our practice around promoting children's wellbeing links to teachers' safeguarding responsibilities. Relationships support wellbeing, so this idea helps to empower learners by giving them autonomy in choosing their trusted grown up in school and at home.

For younger children, this can be run as a whole class discussion and brief drawing task. Older children may wish to engage in more independent reflection and a writing task to document why each person has been identified as a trusted adult.

Begin by discussing with the class that when our wellbeing feels challenged, connecting with others can help. This strategy may already be on your ways to wellbeing review (**Idea 21**) display so there's an option to refer to that. Make a class brainstorm of all the adults known to the children in school and explore the concept of trust. What does it mean to trust someone? How do we know an adult can be trusted? What might we trust someone with?

Explain that it can be helpful to have a trusted adult at school with whom any wellbeing worries or concerns can be shared. Explore the idea that there are lots of grownups on hand to support children's wellbeing as safeguarding is everyone's responsibility. Introduce the idea of children also having the right to choose whom they speak to and encourage them to nominate a trusted grownup in school. Depending on the circumstances of the children, it may be helpful to repeat this idea focussing on people at home or in the community.

Teaching tip

As a teacher, it's important to have real humility here. I've found it interesting how many of my pupils choose the lunchtime supervisor or the school caretaker as their trusted adult; it needn't always be the person with whom they spend most time at school! It's important also to tell the trusted adults they've been identified by learners.

Asking children to identify who their 'go to' adults are can be a simple, reassuring and empowering idea to be used as a reference point when wellbeing support is needed.

What does my hero do?

'Representation matters to us as a school community. This idea helps children see that everyone needs strategies for wellbeing!'
Deputy Headteacher – London, UK

This idea builds on Part 2, in which the importance of destigmatising language related to wellbeing was discussed. Encouraging children to think about the wellbeing of their heroes reinforces the important idea that everybody has wellbeing needs, can face challenges with their wellbeing and deserves support to protect and promote it.

Begin a class discussion about public figures whom the children admire and whom they think are good role models. Encourage a diverse representation of gender, race, age and occupation in the list. Using key questions such as 'What makes them someone to look up to?' or 'What do we know about this person's positive behaviours?', guide the children to justify their choices.

Once the children have co-created a list of key figures, encourage discussion of ways to wellbeing that each person might use to support their physical, emotional or mental health. With older children, this idea presents a great opportunity for independent research which could involve the use of technology, social media or letter writing to try and find out what each key figure identifies as their own strategies to promote and protect their wellbeing. Some teacher-led use of social media platforms such as Twitter may allow children to connect with their favourite musicians/sports figures/authors or role models to learn about their ways to wellbeing.

Consider displaying the research findings as a learning tool. This will help to encourage a clear and secure understanding that our role models need to look after their wellbeing too.

Taking it further

To adapt this idea for use with younger children, you could focus on researching fewer role models as a whole class. Working collaboratively to learn about the author of a favourite book or a local public figure can still reinforce the idea that everyone's wellbeing needs to be looked after. Alternatively, this idea can be connected to topic-based learning about people who help us. Children will enjoy the opportunity to interview senior leaders, other teachers and support staff to find out how they look after their own wellbeing.

What you didn't know!

'A great way to start a new term and get to know each other in an active way! All adults in my class joined in!'
Year 4 Teacher – Yorkshire, UK

This idea is a fun, active opportunity to build connections between learners. It's a good one to try early in your first term.

Begin by setting up clues around the school using the adaptable clues template (available from the online resources). Each clue makes up a square of the nine-square grid used in the second part of the treasure hunt and will include statements such as 'Find someone who has the same number of pets as you' or 'Find someone who likes the same subject as you'. As you hide the clues, make sure you identify on a map where children should look for them. Provide a copy of the treasure hunt map to each pair or trio.

- Challenge the children to find nine statements hidden around the school and regroup in your classroom.
- Put the nine statements together to create a whole class grid template. Explain to the children that you'll complete part two of the 'What you didn't know' challenge the next day.
- Copy the grid so each child has one and challenge children to identify peers in their class who match the statements. You might want to focus on the formulation and articulation of questions before getting started.
- Encourage children to talk to as many peers as they can and to avoid filling their grid with information on friends they know well already.
- Follow up the activity with a whole class task to identify new knowledge about each other and consider how this might be useful in building a class community.

Teaching tip

When you tell children they're off on a hunt around the school, excitement tends to build so remind children of the expectations of moving around school safely!

Bonus idea ★

There's an opportunity to add challenge for older children, asking each child to tally the number of questions asked and the number of people they talk to (this will help diversify the respondents on each grid). Some children will benefit from extended conversations about using the information they find to help them to form friendships. This is a particularly useful starting point for a social intervention conversation; bringing together children with common interests, likes or dislikes can be the beginnings of meaningful classroom connections.

A letter to my buddy

'The excitement of getting post from our buddies was a real motivator for Year 1.'
Head of Year – Dubai, UAE

Many schools use buddy systems effectively to promote a sense of community and connection among learners of all ages. This idea is a cross-curricular learning opportunity which, with some planning, can be used as a whole school activity to build brilliant buddy relationships.

Teaching tip

For older children, it's useful to discuss the responsibilities of being a role model and the opportunities they have in their buddy role to mentor, support and encourage younger learners. For some children, encouraging a sense of responsibility can promote positive feelings of self-worth. Encouraging them to identify positive traits in themselves (such as patience and kindness) can also help to reassure younger buddies.

Taking it further

Once initial letters have been delivered, buddies can respond to one another. They can answer questions they've been asked and begin to build up a picture of each other's interests before meeting in person!

To begin, decide as a staff team which classes and which children will be buddied up together. Ensure all children are accounted for and pupil needs have been carefully considered. Once teachers are all aware of the buddy pairings, year group-specific lessons on letter writing can begin.

Introduce each class to the aims of the buddy system (this will differ depending on the age and stage of the group and you may find the buddy prompts, available from the online resources, a useful guide for this discussion). Brainstorm as a whole class the sorts of things you'd want to share with your buddy in a 'getting to know you' letter. Consider linking to 'I am who I am' (**Idea 55**) as a foundation for this task; a key message for children is that they're unique, special and should share interesting things about themselves.

Using age-appropriate writing frames or scribes if necessary, each child should write an introductory letter to their buddy. Ideally, these could be posted into a school post box by each child, sorted and delivered by Wellbeing Leaders or older children. This tends to be an exciting event for learners as they begin to build connections beyond their classrooms.

Observe and connect

'My placement class needed help to remember what each finger represents but they got so much out of observing pictures carefully and shared great ideas.'
Trainee Primary Teacher – London, UK

This idea helps children to build connections to previous learning and to each other. You need inspiring images, a whiteboard and pen for each child and time for rich discussion.

Show children a photograph and the 'observe and connect hand' (available in the online resources). Get them to draw a hand on their whiteboard and fill in the fingers, starting with the thumb.

1. **Thumb**: 'I see' - children note down what they see in the image.
2. **Index finger**: 'I remember' - children make connections to memories sparked by the image. If it shows a bird flying, a child might remember a story or a connection to science learning and life cycles.
3. **Middle finger**: 'I think' - children identify something they're not sure about, for example, 'I think the bird might be flying for the first time'. Responses to the 'I think' prompt can be a catalyst for critical thinking.
4. **Ring finger**: 'I wonder' - children create enquiry questions. These can be quite open and creative, for example 'I wonder where the bird is flying to?'.
5. **Pinkie finger**: 'I will' - children set a challenge. This might be something as simple as 'I will look out for birds in the playground'.

Teaching tip

This can be a good way to introduce any new concept or topic. It can also be a good morning task for children while they settle in before a register. Ensure that learners work with different partners to help build lots of connections within the class.

Bonus idea ★

Once children have completed their hand outlines by making observations and connections of their own, you could allow time for partner work. Encourage children to share their responses and identify links in their observations.

Lunchtime connection clubs

'The set-up does need some input and commitment from adults but the gains were entirely worthwhile. Lunchtimes are calmer and so much more positive for both children and adults.'
Inclusion Champion (Pastoral Team) – Oxfordshire, UK

Less structured times in the school day (such as break time and lunch time) can be really challenging for some children, particularly if they're facing difficulties with confidence, self-esteem or building relationships. This idea promotes pupil responsibility in older children and allows opportunities for cross-year group connections to be created.

Taking it further

The Connection Club Leaders can be encouraged to create games, put those attending into groups or lead discussions based on the theme of the connection club. Themes could be changed multiple times a week.

Bonus idea ★

It might be helpful to allocate an adult in the playground to observe the initial Connection Clubs and, if necessary, model positive communication skills and inclusive behaviours. Many older children will respond brilliantly to the role and responsibility of being a Connection Club Leader and this should be celebrated and praised.

With a group of older learners, launch the idea of lunchtime connection clubs as an opportunity to combat loneliness. This develops a popular idea of friendship stops or buddy benches in many playgrounds, using a positive focus. Firstly, Connection Club Leaders should work in small groups to identify a theme they are interested in or passionate about. This will need some teacher input to ensure that all learners have something to contribute and that ideas for connection clubs are realistic! They might include activities such as singing, football, Connect 4™, skipping or topic-based interests such as animals, maths or cars. Connection Club Leaders can choose whether they plan games or activities for their allocated days or focus on facilitating discussions among other pupils.

Next, with support from playground supervisors, identify a space where the lunchtime connection club could congregate and display signs with the connection club theme of the day.

In assembly, encourage Connection Club Leaders to explain the purpose and rules of the lunchtime club. Important messaging includes the fact that leaders will help everyone to join in, everyone must be kind and everyone is welcome. .

Linking letters

'We used this as whole school context for writing; the purpose and audience were hugely engaging for learners across all year groups.'
Primary English Lead – London, UK

This idea is designed to connect children with others in their community and aims to promote positive wellbeing by encouraging and fostering self-worth, open-mindedness and curiosity. By building cross-curricular links to writing for different purposes, children can hone their letter-writing skills while learning from those in their community.

In preparation for using this idea, adults in school should make connections with community groups to establish if they would be open to engaging in the linking letters project. Teachers or school office staff could, for example, reach out to care homes for elderly members of the community, contact a community meet-up group designed to combat loneliness or connect with staff or volunteers who are involved with providing support to those who are homeless.

The linking letters idea works best when you start small and keep contact simple. Perhaps choose a celebration or festival as the context. Children could write cards full of well wishes for Christmas or Eid or design firework pictures to celebrate Diwali. Alternatively, they could design and write postcards about a school trip they have been on in the local community. They could also send messages of positivity in recognition of wellbeing week or share letters about their own wellbeing practices in school. It's important that children are helped to understand that they might not receive individual response to their letters. While this is the ideal aim of the activity, expectation management will be important for some children to avoid disappointment.

Taking it further

Where this idea really impacts communities is where opportunities are fostered for ongoing, reciprocal connections. This might involve receiving cards, voice recordings or video messages back from elderly neighbours or a collation of responses to questions about recipients' experiences in the local community. In some settings, it might be possible to arrange for some children to visit the settings or fundraise for charity work within their community.

A woolly web

'This was a great activity to help children make connections and identify similarities with each other. Great when exploring how the children have felt or might feel in different situations.'
Year 2 Teacher – Bali, Indonesia

Creating and maintaining a sense of belonging can promote wellbeing in any classroom. This activity allows children to identify clear connections to each other.

Teaching tip

This activity is a great tool for supporting the inclusion of all learners. It can be particularly effective when new children join a class during the academic year. It can be adjusted to challenge learners by using a theme for the statements. This could include 'Things I like' in Key Stage 1 or statements of belief about any topic in Key Stage 2.

Invite children to join a whole class activity in a sharing circle. It is fun to create a woolly web in the playground but if you want to try it indoors, make extra space around the circle by moving chairs and tables out of the way.

Explore what the children know about webs - how they look, where they've see them, when they appear more noticeable. Emphasise the fact that all webs look different! Explain that the web you're creating is a special woolly web, unique to your class community.

Start by holding the end of a ball of wool and wrap it around your fist so it stays secure. Make a statement which tells the children something about you. For example: 'I have two pets in my house', 'I like pizza' or 'When I'm worried, I like to talk to a friend.' Ask the children to listen and raise their hands if they are connected to you by this statement. Choose one child and throw the ball of wool to them.

The child with the ball of wool holds it and gets ready to make their own statement. Their peers listen and then the person with the wool holds one section and throws the remaining ball of wool to someone who is connected to their statement.

This continues until all children have been connected by their statements.

Bonus idea ★

The same activity could be used as a table task for a small group peer intervention. This can be particularly helpful when building a community or shared commitment to working in a small group of learners from different classes.

Moving and motivating

Part 4

Wiggle time

'An important way to energise and refocus learners of all ages.'
Deputy Headteacher – London, UK

As teachers, we can spot when our learners need to move, stretch or wiggle. This can happen right in the middle of whole class teaching or once learners are absorbed in independent work.

Teaching tip

This can work well for a class who find it tricky to line up calmly and quietly. Once they're in line, calling a ten second wiggle break (which is then followed by still and quiet standing) can help children rediscover their focus.

Taking it further

Encourage one or two learners to take responsibility for instigating wiggle breaks. Children will enjoy the responsibility of this, although some will need limits on how many times a day they can call a wiggle break! Encourage your wiggle monitors to spot when their peers look sleepy or they need to refocus; maintain high expectations for your wiggle monitors to explain their reasons and to enforce the boundaries you established earlier.

Whatever the age and stage of your class, it's important to discuss why we need to allow ourselves to move when we're learning. This can sometimes feel a little counter-intuitive, particularly if your school has behaviour for learning expectations which outline how children should be sitting still. Explaining that stretching, wiggling or moving briefly can help us to reset during the learning process and improve our focus.

It's key to set boundaries on the wiggle time. Specify an agreed amount of wiggle time (around 30 seconds is a good start) and use a visual indicator such as a sand timer to show children how long they have to move. Then, discuss with the children how they can keep themselves (and each other) safe while wiggling. Respecting personal space and not touching other people or classroom furniture while wiggling can be a good starting point for safety expectations. Finally, encourage children to use the full amount of time to wiggle as much as they can and reflect on how it feels during and after their wiggle break.

Word tennis

'An energetic opportunity to share adjective ideas for writing.'
Literacy Specialist – Harrogate, UK

This movement idea can be used as both a learning and a wellbeing tool. All you need is some space, some active imaginations and some good tennis skills. It can be helpful to model this idea to the children; if you have another adult in your classroom, involve them so that the children see first-hand how to play.

- Encourage two opponents to face each other and 'warm up' their tennis skills with an imaginary racket and ball. The children should have enough space to move safely and be encouraged to use their imaginations as they set up to serve or return.
- It can be helpful to use an image to stimulate the first match of word tennis. Try pobble.com for some great stimulus images. Give the children some thinking time while they look at the image and think of adjectives to describe what they see.
- Player 1 serves the imaginary ball to their partner while shouting an adjective to describe the image. Player 2 then returns the serve with a different adjective.
- The game continues in a rally of adjectives until one of the players runs out of words.

Involving the rest of the children in the match is important; they can keep score, be split into teams to cheer for the opponents or, if the players are particularly strong, the crowd could monitor a time limit on their responses so that the play remains fast-paced.

Teaching tip

Children can also act as judges using thumbs up or thumbs down to indicate whether they agree with each player's adjective throughout the game, or write down ideas on whiteboards to support players struggling to think of a word to use.

Taking it further

This is a great game to adapt and apply to lots of different word types and focus areas of the curriculum. To give word tennis a wellbeing focus, try using themed questions related to other teaching points or Personal, Social, Health and Economic Education lessons such as: 'What can I do to help my physical wellbeing?', 'What does a supportive friend do?', 'Where can I get help with my wellbeing?' or 'Which food gives me energy to learn?'.

Vote with your feet

'A great way to encourage children to have opinions about what they're learning.'
Primary 2 Teacher – Fife, UK

This is a great idea to promote critical thinking, reasoning and encourage learners' active engagement at the start of a lesson. Being active at the start sends important messages to learners about engaging throughout a lesson. It can also serve as a great baseline assessment to help teachers to identify key prior knowledge in any curricular area, reveal any misconceptions and challenge learners to reason and justify their thinking.

Teaching tip

If some children find it daunting to commit to a response to big questions and vote with their feet, there are ways to build confidence. Try beginning with simple statements which are low stakes, for example 'Pizza is the best school dinner'. Model reasoning statements and encourage children to think independently. Once children have got used to tackling trickier questions, try using background music to support thinking while they move.

Bonus idea ★

Once your class are used to it, this idea can be useful when exploring sensitive topics such as bullying. Creating a safe, teacher-led space to discuss different viewpoints can positively impact wellbeing.

Begin by displaying 'I agree', 'I disagree', and 'I'm not sure' signs on your classroom walls. Explain to the children that you're going to say a statement, and they'll vote with their feet by going and standing by the sign that represents their opinion. Remind them to move safely within the space, try hard to articulate their own opinions and be ready to justify them if asked. This will take some practice as children may follow their peers or provide the answer they think the teacher wants to hear! Praise and positive reinforcement should be given to children who think independently and justify their choice, even if, as teachers, we don't agree with them.

As with word tennis (**Idea 32**), vote with your feet can be used in different ways across the curriculum. Checking for knowledge and understanding through fact recall from a science lesson or checking for misconceptions around a maths topic, can be an engaging way to encourage active learning. This can be a particularly good idea to use when addressing challenges with social interactions and friendships. Using statements to prompt debate can allow children to assert their views and then begin to understand other perspectives.

Mirror me

'This simple movement task helped children develop collaboration and concentration skills!'
Teaching Assistant – London, UK

This movement idea groups learners into trios with each child taking on an important role of actor, mirror or observer. It's designed to be a silent movement idea which can be tailored to the energy levels of your class and the space available for movement.

It can be interesting to begin this activity without a great deal of teacher input as children often learn best from experiencing the challenges of leading or following actions first hand.

- To begin, split children into groups of three and assign roles. The actor and the mirror face one another and the observer sits close to them, with a good view of the action.
- The observer should watch carefully as the actor moves their body and the mirror follows and replicates the movements at the same time.
- After a brief try without any guidance, stop and ask for observer feedback. Questions to support the discussion could include: 'When did things get tricky for your mirror?' and 'What could the actor do to support the mirror?'.
- Encourage the observer to set a target for improvement for their teammates.
- Repeat the movement activity and see if both learners can respond to their observer's target.
- Take feedback again from the observers and hopefully they will identify improvement.

The aim of this activity is around awareness, focus and noticing as well as mindful, conscious movement. Children will enjoy the opportunity to try out different roles and reflect on what they find hardest or most enjoyable.

Teaching tip

With the right expectations for a quiet environment and gentle, calm movement, this can be a good idea for resetting and preparing for focussed learning.

Taking it further

This idea could fit well in some drama lessons and, if resources are available, some children will learn a lot from filming and watching each other's mirror me work. Using a sample film can provide a great stimulus for developing supportive, specific peer assessment language too.

Yes! Let's!

'Seeing children feeling empowered by their peers' responses and watching them engage so creatively is brilliant!'
Primary 2 Teacher – Fife, UK

By combining an opportunity for a movement break, some physical activity and creative thought, this strategy allows children to become imaginative leaders in learning. It works best with lots of space so a gym or playground would be perfect.

Teaching tip

This is a great game to target descriptive language in an active, empowering way. Try giving the activity a theme and challenging children to use adverbs, adjectives or to choose nouns particularly connected to their learning.

Begin to warm up by exploring big movements and small movements in a circle. Try a simple 'my turn, your turn' mirroring activity to make sure children are noticing and following a leader's change in movement.

Next it's time to provide an opportunity for individual expression while still staying on a spot in the circle. Give a simple instruction encouraging children to use their bodies in different ways to represent an action or an object related to a topic being taught in class – or it could be completely unrelated. For example: 'Build a wall using heavy bricks!' or 'Climb out of your space ship and carefully walk on to the moon's surface!'.

Now it's time to move in the circle. Practise call and response where the leader says, 'Let's be...' and the followers respond, 'Yes, let's!'.

Start with the teacher saying 'Let's be...' and modelling lots of descriptive language and creativity, for example: 'Let's be elephants with long trunks stomping through mud!'. The children respond with 'Yes, let's!' and then create their own version of the action.

The game progresses with children as the leaders, shouting out their 'Let's be...' idea and passing on their role to a peer by tapping them on the shoulder so they can share their creativity.

Big feelings, big movements

'This activity was very effective to support the children with self-regulation and those learning English as second language.'
Grade 1 Teacher – Dubai, UAE

This idea supports children to develop an understanding of how emotions and feelings might be experienced physically. Encouraging children to build connections between their physical and emotional wellbeing can really develop an awareness of indicators and a capacity to use strategies to address challenges independently.

- Ask children to sit in a circle and choose a volunteer to start the activity.
- The volunteer moves to the centre of the circle and picks a card from the stack. The card shows a feeling word and, if appropriate, a visual representation of the feeling with a facial expression.
- The child hides the card and then uses movement and facial expressions to act out the feeling. Peers are given time to think, confer and decide on which feeling they think is being shown by the child in the centre.
- Next, the teacher leads a conversation on how your body might tell you that you were feeling that particular emotion. For example, if the card says angry, ask the children 'What happens to the inside or outside of your body when you feel angry?' or 'What was the last thing that made you angry?'.
- Finally, all children get a chance to use their own big movements to show big feelings. As with all movement activities, it's important to establish ground rules around safe movement. This part of the activity allows for creativity as children can express how an emotion feels in their body with big movement. Some children will benefit from teacher modelling or visuals to support them.

> ### Taking it further
>
> An extension to this can help children to identify feelings after the circle game. Noting children's ideas of how each emotion feels in their body can create a useful reference point for self-regulation. For example, if children suggest that anger feels like 'a volcano in my tummy' or 'hotness in my face', this can be noted on a brainstorm for 'angry' and referred to if that emotion emerges for the child later.

A positive snowstorm

'We love the snowstorm as a fun way to share ideas.'
Grade 1 Teacher – Dubai, UAE

A fun, active wellbeing activity, this positive snowstorm needs scrap paper, plenty of space and some discussions about safe snowball throwing before getting started!

I've used this idea frequently with trainee teachers as a way to introduce Personal, Social, Health and Economic Education topics; we often talk about how it's a non-threatening way for children to get to share ideas anonymously. Promoting pupil voice can support self-esteem, confidence and emotional wellbeing and this is an exciting, albeit unusual, way to ensure even our quietest learners are heard.

Children are given a topic to write about on a piece of paper. They then crumple up the page into a snowball! The active part involves a whole class snowball fight. This often works best with some accompanying high energy music and a time limit. Some children will need to be reminded to keep picking up and throwing new snowballs rather than catching and immediately opening one. When the music stops or the time expires, make sure everyone has a snowball to open and read.

This activity can be used to share ideas as a baseline introduction to any new topic. For a wellbeing-focussed snowstorm, children could write a positive, encouraging message before a test or big event like a class assembly. If you're learning about ways to stay physically active, children could write a list of ideas for a one-minute movement challenge. If there are any issues with friendships in your classroom, children could write as many characteristics of a good friend as they can.

Bonus idea ★

Another way to use the positive snowstorm is to make each snowball personalised to an individual in the class. For this, provide each child with a sheet of paper with another classmate's name on it. Leave these face-down at each desk before introducing the snowstorm and encourage them to keep the names secret. They then write three positive things about their peer. For some children, this will need a bit of teacher-led discussion to make sure feedback is kind and supportive. Children don't have to end up with their own snowball of compliments but will often enjoy listening to others read out a positive list about them.

Heartbeats and hopes

'We incorporated this into our science learning on the circulatory system, which was a fantastic way to link wellbeing across our curriculum. After the initial task, children started using this activity to cool down after playtime. Keeping a wellbeing journal has allowed children to track and reflect on how their hope changes.'
Year 6 Teacher – Dubai, UAE

This idea can be adapted to help combine physical activity, an understanding of heart rates and a chance for quiet reflection on hopes and aspirations.

- Firstly, encourage children to find their heartbeat by placing their fingers on their wrist or the side of their neck. For this part of the task, encourage learners to be quiet and focus very carefully on feeling and noticing their heartbeat. Set a timer for a minute and encourage learners to count how many times their heart beats in a minute, if they can.
- Next, pair children up and sit them opposite each other. One child is responsible for counting 60 heart beats while the other thinks about a hope they have. Some children may like to close their eyes to focus on their hope and may also be comfortable sharing their hope with their partner.
- Swap roles so that every child has a chance to think about a hope. This can be a positive, calming way for children to set intentions and refocus before a lesson or after a high energy break time or active lesson.

You can extend this activity by completing some brief, vigorous exercise and returning to measure heartbeats, noticing changes in our bodies and number of beats each minute. Children can choose the movement and lead their peers for a minute before returning to the quiet heartbeat measuring part of the idea.

Taking it further

Some children will enjoy taking note of (and returning to reflect on) their hopes. If possible, allowing children to keep a wellbeing journal can be a powerful way for them to track strategies for wellbeing and to notice their progress in relation to hopes or goals they've set.

Mood mover

'This activity allowed children to develop leadership skills and become more aware of how their moods can change after movement. The wellbeing trackers allowed children to reflect on which movements they prefer whilst the menu also promotes pupil choice.'
Personal, Social, Health and Economic Education Lead – Dubai, UAE

This idea encourages children to identify how they want to feel and then take action to find that feeling through engagement in movement or with a wellbeing strategy. It builds on other ideas in the book and can be part of a bigger unit of learning through Personal, Social, Health and Economic Education about the impact of movement for physical and mental health.

Teaching tip

To help all children to engage with this idea, it can be helpful to set some ground rules and expectations for behaviour. There may be a need to focus particularly on engagement or responding positively to others' participation.

Using this idea as a whole school initiative for a particular block of time (a month's challenge for example) can be particularly impactful. It's key that everyone is involved and that children see teachers and other adults joining in with the mood mover scheduled moments. An initial teaching focus should be identifying different moods or feelings which may come up; these discussions can be tailored to specific stages of development and may also reflect year-group specific challenges or events (such as transitions, preparations for assessments or new responsibilities). Linking to Big feelings, big movements (**Idea 36**) may support children to remember how physical sensations communicate a feeling or emotion.

You could begin by reflecting as a whole class on the sorts of feelings the children have been experiencing and how they were able to identify them. It can really help the children to access this discussion if you are able to share some of your own experiences. This might include something as simple as feeling 'butterflies' in your stomach when you're excited or noticing a faster heartbeat when you're worried about something.

Next, design a menu of movements for the classroom (keeping in mind the limitations of the physical learning environment). Make sure all the movements on the menu are ones which the children feel will help to energise them/bring calm/release stress/wake up their minds for learning. When identifying feelings or moods and designing a menu of movement options, it's vital that children feel a sense of autonomy and choice. The menu can be updated as and when you or the children notice that some new movements would support engagement and motivation.

At a set time daily, every class stops to assess their mood and children decide which movement from the menu to use as a response. In some classes, it will work well for a child to become the mood mover monitor; they could be given the responsibility for identifying the mood in the room and choosing from the menu on behalf of their peers. In other classrooms, however, there is a need for individual responses to wellbeing and it's really key to give children the chance to respond independently. If you opt for individual responses and to promote pupil autonomy, there may be several different movements happening in your classroom at the same time. Grouping children together who are using the same movement may be helpful to keep everyone focussed.

This idea can also work well in the playground. When children have more space in which to move, they may also require a broader range of movements to choose from. Perhaps consider developing an indoor movement menu and an outdoor adaptation.

Taking it further

Once children have tried and tested their menus, use the learning experience as a cross-phase peer teaching opportunity to raise the profile of mood movement in school. Try also to weave in small mood movement opportunities during whole school assemblies.

Mind/movement monitors

'The monitors are so good at spotting when we need to stop and move!'
Early Career Teacher – London, UK

This pupil-led physical activity allows children to initiate moments of movement in the classroom. It can also be used to reinforce learning developed through PE and can allow individual children (or small groups) to become mind/movement leaders.

Taking it further

If children are keeping a wellbeing journal, they can log and track progress of the movement challenge in it. Some children might benefit also from repeating the movement challenge more than once during the school day to compare their energy levels or results. There is also an opportunity to build in partner work to this idea. Pairing children up and allocating one child the role of the mover and the other the role of the encourager (and then swapping) can increase energy, camaraderie and motivation.

An important aspect of using this idea is to consider how much choice you can give to the children. Will you set a movement break time in your daily timetable or will children themselves identify when they need to move in order to learn better? In some classes, if learning behaviour and self-awareness are high on the agenda, nominated monitors could choose when a movement break is needed. In others, it might be useful to build a one-minute challenge into a visual timetable so that children can see they'll have an opportunity to move within the day.

Once the timing of the movement opportunity has been decided, a nominated leader (or small group of leaders) introduces the movement to their peers. It can be helpful for a teacher to suggest an alternative action to ensure all children are included in the challenge. After making sure everyone is clear on the movement, set a one-minute timer and challenge your class to repeat it as many times as they can in the minute. There may be an opportunity to count how many times the movement is repeated (for example, if star jumps or squats are chosen). Alternatively, if leaders choose an action such as running on the spot, children are challenged to keep going without stopping for the whole minute.

Cultivating a culture of care

Part 5

Care treasure map

'Providing children with a map to guide their choices supports them to find a solution and become more independent.'
Learning Support Assistant – Surrey, UK

This can be a fun project to extend children's learning about self-care and how to support their own wellbeing. Whilst creating a care treasure map, children will reflect on the merits and challenges of their self-care strategies (and hopefully learn new ones from each other). It's also a great opportunity for them to reflect on the school environment, their indoor and outdoor surroundings, and to think about where they can promote and protect their wellbeing in school.

Teaching tip

This idea can be used as a cross-curricular project where children investigate their surroundings, make observations and create maps of their local environment. It might also lead to some community action or environmental improvement if children identify opportunities for innovation. (For example, they might identify a space which is not being used efficiently and could be turned into a sensory zone or gardening space).

Taking it further

Peer sharing can extend the learning opportunities – try buddying up classes to share their care treasure maps.

Give each child access to a map of their school environment (older children may create this map themselves as part of a geography unit, whereas younger children may use a simple version created for them). Look at the map together and encourage children to share their own favourite places at school in a pair or small group discussion. Through questioning, support children to explore why a particular space in the school environment might be preferable over another. Themes such as space, noise levels, nature or autonomy might emerge in this discussion.

Next, encourage children to share self-care strategies they use, related to spaces around the school. These might include going to a quiet corner of the playground and listening for birdsong, taking time to notice the colours and scents of flowers in a playground garden or seeking out a reading space somewhere comfortable in the library. Record these ideas as the initial thoughts which could be added to each child's personal care treasure map.

Next, allow the children to explore the environment and record, through lists or photographs, places where they or other children could engage in self-care activities. Children will often notice opportunities which adults haven't spotted and it is important to accept and celebrate the individuality of responses. It's good for learners to understand that choice and personal preferences are key when addressing our own wellbeing needs. What's good for my self-care and therefore valid on my care treasure map might be different from what's good for yours!

Regroup in the classroom and share ideas; encouraging children to magpie ideas from each other is useful here as some children will find the idea of self-care practices difficult to access. Finally, children add their ideas to their map of the environment and create their personalised care treasure map. They can then refer to this as an independent strategy for self-care. It is useful for children to store their care treasure maps somewhere accessible. Adults in school can then remind learners of their independently created resource when self-care becomes a priority.

Bonus idea

This could be extended into a home learning task. Encouraging children to reflect on their local environment and think about places which support their self-care can be a useful and thought-provoking extension. They could also be asked to create a collaborative care map with parents, carers or their siblings.

Care commitment

'A child-led care commitment is the foundation for understanding boundaries and directing positive choices.'
Year 3 Teacher – Dubai, UAE

Engaging children in the creation of a class charter is a common way to promote responsibility and collective accountability in the learning environment. This idea creates a commitment to putting care at the centre of a class charter and its language.

Teaching tip

Suggestions for both categories might include:

We care for: ourselves, our friends, visitors to our classroom, our uniforms, our library books.
We care about: being kind, fair, honest, doing our best in learning.

Taking it further

The care commitment can be a working document with additional statements added in response to particular issues which emerge within or beyond your classroom community. If global events prompt concern and associated action by your pupils, 'We care about our role as global citizens' could be added. On a smaller scale, if there are issues within the classroom, things like 'We care about looking after pen lids!' may be useful additions.

At the start of an academic year, begin discussing the word 'care'. Encourage the children to name ways in which they have seen people being caring and why care might be important in their new classroom. If possible, record responses in a word cloud or brainstorm so that you can use them in the care commitment.

Explore the idea of contracts and commitment; explain that every person who works in the school signs a contract to confirm how they promise to behave. Present the idea of a care commitment as a form of contract or shared vision of how the classroom environment should feel for everyone.

Using the headings 'In Class X we care for... .' (focus on tangible items or people) and 'In Class X we care about... .' (focus on topics, themes or behaviours), agree a list of statements relevant to your class. Asking questions such as 'How would you know someone cared about learning?' can explain to children how each of the care commitment statements might work in practice.

Once the children have agreed on the most important statements, display them somewhere clear for the children to see. They could even be asked to sign to agree to them.

Looks like, sounds like, feels like

'Breaking down the three elements of a positive classroom allows children to really dissect their understanding.'
Year 3 Teacher – London, UK

This idea is a simple way to establish expectations for a safe and positive learning environment. It can be used at the start of term with a new class or as a responsive approach to promoting wellbeing when things become challenging in your classroom.

With your class sitting in a circle, show them three large hoops in the middle of the floor. Label one 'looks like', one 'sounds like' and one 'feels like'. Ask them to think about their ideal learning environment. Address each hoop in turn: 'What does your ideal learning environment look like?' Encourage the children to share ideas within a pair or trio, then to agree on a top priority, add it to a sticky note and put it in the hoop. Repeat this for each hoop ('What does your ideal learning environment sound like?', 'What does your ideal learning environment feel like?') and then work with the children to identify themes.

This idea can be a good way to get to know the diversity of wants and needs of your learners at the start of a new academic year. Ideally, adults in the room should also contribute to the hoops to demonstrate a sense of community. If there are increased conflicts or challenges in behaviour for learning in your class it's also a good idea to come back to this activity when required. As with many of the other ideas in the book, creating a visible display to refer to when necessary can be helpful for some learners.

Bonus idea ★

While the collaborative discussion in this idea helps children to reflect on how their ideas may differ but also connect, this can also be a useful tool to use with individuals. If you have a new arrival midway through the term, it can be useful to capture some thinking from them and then refer to it as you support them to settle in. It can also be an interesting adaptation to a one-page profile as it allows children to think about their environment as impactful on their own wellbeing and readiness to learn.

Community action week

'There was a buzz in our school when missions were launched. The children were so proud of making changes to their community.'
Year 2 Teacher – Singapore

This whole school initiative helps children to learn that there are many opportunities to become active and effective contributors to the wider community. By starting small and acting within the school, young learners can be empowered to take on their own projects. The aim of the week is for every class to engage in one small action to help or bring joy to other members of the school community.

Teaching tip

It's important to document the actions with lots of photographs and encourage children to reflect on their participation after the week. Make sure the voices of those who are impacted by the positive actions are also captured!

Taking it further

A whole school approach to community action can be the catalyst for individuals or small groups of motivated learners to design and carry out their own projects. Where possible, encourage this initiative and celebrate the positive impact.

Start by deciding, as a staff, on a week of the school calendar which can be community action week. Ideally, it would be during the first term as this allows opportunities to extend to more independent, child-led community action thereafter. Next, work together as a staff group to brainstorm action ideas which can be allocated to each class. This will need some creative thinking and it will also be important to consider the logistics and resourcing of projects.

Start small and consider simple, low-resource actions such as litter picking, gardening or sorting library books. While tangible responsibilities like sorting resources in an outdoor learning space will work well for some children, not all actions need to have a product or outcome focus. Think about spreading joy as another way to engage in community action; a class could take responsibility for baking treats for support staff or for making thank you cards for cleaners and caretakers.

To raise the profile of community action week, try launching the theme in a whole school assembly. Explain to the children that each class will receive notice of their community action mission; this tends to increase excitement when envelopes arrive in classrooms and plans begin!

Self-care showcase

'The buzz for self-care could be felt across the school. Children (and staff) couldn't wait to exchange ideas!'
Wellbeing Lead – London, UK

This idea requires a whole school approach. The showcase should be displayed somewhere prominent, such as in a cafeteria.

Launch the idea of a whole school self-care showcase in assembly. Adding 'work in progress' signs to the area you plan to display the showcase can build excitement among children as they work on the space.

Initially, children will share self-care strategies in their classes. Using themes of physical, mental, social, spiritual and environmental wellbeing can provide a useful structure. Consider colour-coding each theme for the final display.

Encourage children to document their strategy through drawing or writing, noting which dimension of wellbeing it relates to and how it impacts them. Using the format (available from the online resources), each child completes their own contribution to the whole school display. If possible, photograph children using their specific self-care strategy and then write a brief explanation underneath. Back each of the strategies on paper which corresponds to the colour code for the theme. There should be a range of themes from each class.

On the display space, group contributions into the dimensions of wellbeing and then also by each class or year group. This can really help children to find their own work easily and to identify which class other contributors are from.

A key requirement of this idea is that children get a chance to visit the self-care showcase regularly and are encouraged to borrow and use ideas from peers across the school.

Taking it further

You might involve parents, carers and families by asking them to add to the display and encouraging them to take inspiration from each other by borrowing self-care ideas from the wider community.

Bonus idea

It can be powerful for children to see adults engaging in wellbeing practices. By modelling proactive approaches to self-care, we support learners to see that their self-care strategies will be relevant beyond their time in school. Children are often fascinated to see photos of their headteacher out running or their playground supervisors looking after a pet. These insights can be the stimulus for powerful discussions about wellbeing which may lead to trusted professional relationships being built.

Need to have, nice to have

'An important reminder of responsibilities, wants and needs.'
Year 2 Teacher – London, UK

This idea helps children to care for their learning environment and have ownership over its set up. All you need is a big piece of paper divided into two columns for each table and some markers.

Taking it further

If you adopt the care crew (**Idea 48**) idea in your classroom, those elected as crew members could take responsibility for reminding their peers about the responsibilities identified in the 'nice to have' columns. Displaying up to ten agreed priorities somewhere prominent can help this idea to create sustainable change.

Ask children to notice what's in their classroom environment by listing as many things as they can. A fun way to do this is to sit in a circle and challenge the children to each say one thing – how many times can you go round the circle before they get stuck? Then ask them to think about the difference between needs and wants. This is a chance to link to some global citizenship learning and perhaps refer to images you used in Spot the similarities (**Idea 80**).

Make a list of what the class believe they need to have in their classroom to help them learn. This might take some guidance as some learners will find it difficult to make the distinction between necessity and luxury.

Begin to make the connection between need to have and nice to have. If the children identify that we need books to write in to record our learning, discuss that it is nice to keep these tidy and stored safely in the right place. If they identify that they need glue sticks, guide them to see that it is nice for them to last as long as possible so it's vital to keep the lids on them when they're not being used.

After a whole class discussion, give the children some time to work on this in small groups. It is often interesting to observe the differences in the lists when they're child-initiated rather than adult-led.

Not random acts of kindness (NRAOK)

'Children loved taking responsibility for their NRAOK. It really helped to embed a consistent ethos of kindness within the classroom and beyond.'
Wellbeing Lead – London, UK

Many schools use random acts of kindness to promote positivity. This idea makes this approach more intentional and planned.

This idea needs a coordinator who will be the recipient of each class's NRAOK. In order to help build relationships and embed this idea, maintain allocations for NRAOK for at least a month. Announcing the pairings of classes for NRAOK works well in some settings, but you may prefer to keep the organisers of each NRAOK secret until the end of the month and allow children to guess before a big reveal.

An assembly launch ensures all children and staff are aware of the intended outcomes of this approach. Discuss ways in which kindness could be shown by one class to another in a thoughtful, intentional way. Encourage the children to share ideas which could fit into a school day. These might include organising a playtime game for another group of children or making surprise treats.

To work well, the frequency of NRAOK should be agreed by staff, although pupil voice and choice should be at the centre of their planning. To maintain the focus on 'not random', the acts of kindness should be carefully planned, so children may need to research their recipients to ensure meaningful, useful gestures. For example, if one class is learning about growing and changing, their partner class might send a parcel of seeds.

Teaching tip

In order to make it clear that a surprise or small gesture is a NRAOK, a bright and clear label could be attached or printed onto any letters/postcards written.

Taking it further

This idea could be extended so that each class is responsible for another class and also for an identified member of staff. Children also respond positively to having responsibility for sharing kindness with a trusted adult; especially when the recipient responds with excitement and gratitude!

Care crew

'The care crew are very proactive in our breaktimes, it's great to see them leading so confidently.'
Playground Supervisor – London, UK

This idea works similarly to a student council. It allows different children to work together to promote the value of care in the school community. It doesn't require complex resources and just needs some adult-led discussion and training for its young members.

Taking it further

Changing the care crew members every term or half term allows more children to be involved. It might be helpful to write a child-friendly care crew job description so that all members know what is and what isn't their responsibility.

Bonus idea ★

Inviting the care crew to a monthly meeting with senior leadership so that they can feed back on what they've seen, or what they feel is needed to make the school a more caring place, can really promote pupil voice. Some care crew members take this very seriously and bring convincing arguments to senior leaders.

As a whole school initiative, each class nominates two pupils each term to be part of the care crew. Those nominated should be identified within their classrooms as being caring, understanding of the needs of others and ready for responsibility. Once elected, they should be introduced at a whole school assembly and be easily identifiable by other learners. Depending on the school's size, this could be through a small display of photographs or through allocation of care crew high-vis vests for during break and lunchtimes.

The remit for the care crew can be specific to your setting; in some schools the care crew work closely with the wellbeing lead to come up with ideas to promote mental health awareness, in others they are more focussed on celebrating positive play and careful use of equipment in the playground. It's important that the care crew are clear that it's not their job to apply the school's behaviour policy but rather that they should be positive role models and actively notice the care demonstrated by their peers in different learning spaces.

Memory box

'This was a meaningful experience for the child in so many ways. The gathering and bringing together of special memories and objects seemed to help the child to talk openly about their thoughts, feelings and emotions regarding their loss.'
Special Educational Needs Coordinator – London, UK

Cultivating a culture of care is important for all children, but there are points in any person's life where extra care can provide support through difficult times. When working with children who have experienced a bereavement, this simple idea can provide an opportunity to reflect on, share and preserve special memories of a loved one. Ideally, this should be a 1:1 task with a trusted adult.

Begin by covering and decorating a special box; allow the child to choose the materials they would like to use and the way they would like the box to look. Discuss the idea that a memory box can be a special collection of key items which remind us of a person who has died. Depending on the age of the child and their understanding of grief, it may be helpful to explore a memory box as a personal, positive reminder of someone special which they can revisit to help them.

Next, discuss what they'd like to keep in the memory box and why each item holds relevance. If this idea is being used in school, it might help the child to write a list of the items they'd like to collect for their box so that they can gather them at home or draw representations of particular memories.

If possible, encourage the child to write a note of what each item represents (scribe for them if appropriate). The list can then be stored in the memory box to help with their recollection of special moments and objects later in their grief journey.

Taking it further

An adaptation of this idea is useful if you ever experience the death of a pupil in your class. I have seen similar approaches being used as part of pastoral support. A classroom memory box has been created and each child has been invited to share memories of their classmate and add it to the box. It may also be appropriate to share the memory box with the child's family.

Treasure chest

'The children were so motivated to look after instruments and resources once we set up the treasure chest.'
Primary Music Specialist – Melbourne, Australia

Combining positive praise and celebration of caring behaviours with a tangible incentive can help some learners to maintain focus on remaining mindful of others in the learning environment. This is particularly helpful for younger children but can also work well in older classes where inconsistencies in caring behaviours occur.

Teaching tip

Before the treasure chest idea begins in your classroom, take some time to work with the children to share ideas of how they could be caring towards each other, the environment and themselves. Build in some reflection time at the end of the initial days of using the treasure chest to make sure it gets a high profile.

You will need a treasure chest (which can be a recycled shoe box or a wooden box if one is available) and golden coins (onto which children's names and details of their caring actions can be noted).

Begin by introducing the treasure chest to the children in a circle time activity. Try Observe and connect (**Idea 27**) to promote pupils' curiosity before introducing the purpose of the care treasure chest. Explain to the children that throughout the term, you and all other adults in the classroom will be actively trying to spot behaviour which is caring. Each time a child is noticed showing care for another learner, taking care of property in the classroom or using self-care strategies, their name will be added to a golden coin (with a short description of the observation) and the coin will be carefully stored in the treasure chest.

Bonus idea ★

Once the children are used to adults identifying actions of care in the classroom, they could be invited to nominate others to receive golden coins.

At the end of the term, the teacher or wellbeing lead will choose a coin (or multiple coins) from the treasure chest at random and those children win a prize. Engaging the children in deciding what the prize could be will help to motivate them but, in my experience, this needs some expectation management!

Supporting
self-esteem

Part 6

IDEA 51

Ask an expert

'Allowing our children to value and celebrate their differences has improved their motivation and self-belief. Ultimately this helped them be more supportive of each other's needs and strengths.'
Year 4 Teacher – Berkshire, UK

Encouraging children to identify their strengths can support wellbeing. Not only does this activity promote self-esteem for learners, it can also facilitate independence and resourcefulness.

Teaching tip

This idea works best when the experts are signposted to other learners at the relevant time, for example, if children are struggling to navigate playground relationships – call on the playground games experts!

Bonus idea ★

Simple 'ask an expert' signs in moveable picture frames can be placed on the desks of experts during relevant lessons. This will provide both a self-esteem boost for the expert and a good visual reminder for peers who might approach them for help.

This idea works best once you've had some time to get to know your class and they also have a sense of each other's skills and qualities. In circle time (ideally at the start of the day) introduce the idea of an expert mission. Ask the children to remember the person sitting on their left. Throughout the day, they should spot something that their neighbour is really good at. It might help to take a photo of the circle in case children need reminders of who they're observing. At the end of the same day, reform the circle and ask children to share observations about their neighbour. Continue the discussion by asking each child to reflect on whether they agree with what their neighbour says they are expert at or whether there's something else they think they're really good at. Introduce the idea of class experts as an opportunity to celebrate differences, use our strengths and create a happy learning community.

Make a list of the areas of expertise identified by the class and work together to nominate at least two experts per area. The list might include experts in number, phonics, addition, manners, lining up, playground games, lunch hall, punctuation or lost property. Display the expert categories somewhere accessible and agree how often nominated experts will change roles. Ideally, everyone should be identified as an expert in something.

Kindness tree

'Trying this with my class really changed the mood in the room! They were so excited to share their kindness and now they independently recognise how to establish a kinder classroom environment.'
Trainee Primary Teacher – London, UK

Reinforcing the importance of growth and change is an important element of promoting wellbeing in the primary classroom. This visual display celebrates kindness and encourages children to observe as their classroom becomes a kinder place to learn!

Before introducing this activity to your class, you will need a tree trunk and branches outline for a display and a good supply of leaf shapes.

- As a class, explore how being kind helps us grow as individuals and as a community. Encourage children to share recollections of when a peer or staff member was kind to them and the impact it had.
- To launch the kindness tree, explore different ways to show kindness with the children. You could display these ideas as roots of your tree. Make them as varied as possible.
- Give each child a leaf with a classmate's name on it. If your class are older, they may be able to keep their nominated peer a secret for a 'big reveal' once the leaf gets added to the tree.
- Agree a time frame during which each child should try and catch their classmate being kind. This works well over the course of at least two or three days so there's plenty of time for everyone to demonstrate kindness!
- Identify some time for children to fill in their leaf (or tell an adult who can scribe for them). They should try to explain on the leaf both what happened and what the impact of the kindness was.
- Add all the leaves to the kindness tree.

Taking it further

Ideally, your classroom kindness tree can become a permanent feature. Once children have got used to catching each other being kind, they can be given the responsibility of designing and adding leaves to the tree independently. Encouraging other adults in the school to add to the tree will raise its profile in your classroom. The kindness tree can be a great reminder when challenging behaviour or conflict occurs.

30 reasons why we love

'Our classroom became a different environment when our children learnt how to respect and celebrate diversity as well as to have and show compassion for others.'
Year 4 Teacher – Berkshire, UK

This is a great idea for building self-esteem, celebrating diversity and encouraging peer reflections in your classroom. I initially discovered this on Twitter and found it a good way to end the week on a positive note!

Teaching tip

If you think learners need some modelling, do an example involving a colleague. Identifying 30 things your class love about a teaching assistant, caretaker or lunchtime supervisor can spread joy and positively impact an adult's wellbeing too!

The aim of this activity is to surround a child's outline with 30 reasons why they are loved (edit the number depending on how many children and adults are part of your classroom community!).

- Choose one child at the end of each week (keep a note of who is chosen so that everyone gets a turn) and ask them to stand in front of the whiteboard. You may wish to use this idea combined with a behaviour incentive such as 'star of the week'.
- Encourage the child to strike a pose and draw round their outline on the board. If it's an option, they could then sit in a special chair or in front of the class while they listen to positive feedback from their peers.
- Get the rest of the class to say a reason why this child is loved. Encourage them to be creative and make sure you give thinking time. There may be some children who find it hard to identify things they love about a peer so be ready to model some ideas! Depending on the age of your pupils, encourage them to think about positive attributes that explore the whole person.
- Add each statement to the board around the child's outline (and include the name of the person who shared the feedback).

Bonus idea

Once all the ideas have been written on the board around the child's outline, ask them to stand back inside their outline and take a photo. These photos of children surrounded by reasons why they're loved can make affordable, meaningful and memorable end of year gifts.

Looking back, facing forward

'These personalised reflections hung in our class all year and were a super reminder of progress for the children.'
Assistant Headteacher – Dubai, UAE

Reflecting and target setting help children develop a positive sense of themselves as learners. This idea is best for older learners and involves partner work. Try it when you're meeting a new class.

In this idea you'll create a hanging display of profiles reminding learners where they have come from and what they are aiming for this academic year. You can see some example photos on the online resources site.

- Partner the children and provide each pair with two A3 sheets of black paper, four white A4 sheets and some chalk. Fix the first partner's black paper onto the wall and ask the child to stand in front of it, facing sideways. The second child then chalks around their partner's profile. Encourage the model to stay as still as possible; this may take multiple attempts and prompt much laughter! Swap roles, and once each child is happy with their chalk profile, they cut it out.
- Discuss the value of looking back on previous learning to recognise progress. Pairs work together to create a list of achievements from the previous school year, one for each of them, and write them under the title 'Looking back', on the white paper.
- Then move the discussion to target setting. Explore the importance of holistic goals which encompass academic learning, social interactions and personal interests. Each child creates a list of targets on their white paper under the heading 'Facing forward'.
- Stick the list of reflections on one side of the profile and goals on the other, and hang the profiles from the ceiling.

Teaching tip

Remember that children may need support from peers and adults to create their targets. This activity also works well for setting individual behaviour targets. Through pupil/teacher conferencing, each child could co-create a behaviour target they are committed to achieving. The display then acts as a clear reminder of self-identified expectations.

I am who I am

'My students loved the creative element which really allowed them time to consider who they are and what's important to them. This has given them greater insight into what they personally need to achieve and to be the best they can be!'
Youth Coach – Edinburgh, UK

This cross-curricular art and English lesson idea is a great context for encouraging reflection and developing self-worth. Artwork and a poem combined create a simple, unique and celebratory visual representation of each child's self-esteem.

Teaching tip

Pair work and group discussions can really help generate ideas. Mind maps could include ideas such as 'I am a learner', 'I am a sister', 'I am a football player'. With some teacher modelling, encourage children to think about themselves (positively) in more abstract ways like 'I am an encourager', 'I am hopeful' or 'I am a change maker'.

Bonus idea ★

If space allows, displaying completed 'I am who I am' poetry can be a great celebration of diversity in the classroom.

Children should begin by designing the background for their 'I am who I am' poetry. Give each child a piece of white paper and share an example of some completed background designs. Give children a choice of pale coloured paints and complete freedom to design the background for their writing. Explain that their poetry will be written on their background painting so blocks of colour will work best. On another piece of paper or whiteboard ask children to create a mind map around their own name with ideas for completing the statement 'I am...'. Encourage creative thinking here to prompt concrete and abstract ideas.

Once children have all generated their ideas, encourage some peer interaction to develop the mind maps. Give children sticky notes and ask them to visit other groups' mind maps and make additions. For example, if they notice a friend has used predominantly concrete statements and might need help to see their positive traits, children can add ideas of characteristics to celebrate.

Encourage children to pick their top five favourite 'I am' statements to turn into their poem. Get them to write a draft then copy the final version onto their painted background using black marker.

Register affirmations

'The children learned to love this opportunity. Staff have been so inspired by the children's commitment to believing in and seeing the positives in themselves!'
Inclusion Lead – London, UK

Using register time as an opportunity to model and encourage positive self-talk can set learners up for the day. This simple idea uses positive affirmations as a register response and encourages children to reflect on their strengths.

When calling the register, encourage each of the children to respond to their name by sharing a positive affirmation about themselves with their peers. If necessary, allow children who aren't comfortable sharing their affirmation with the whole class to share theirs with a chosen peer. Confidence will increase the more this approach is used.

Before using such affirmations, it's useful to introduce the idea of positive self-talk as a tool to help children develop self-esteem. This might be as simple as a circle time discussion about kindness and an encouragement to use kind words for ourselves and others. Older children might be able to relate the use of affirmations to their mindsets for learning and can be helped to understand that affirming their strengths can support the development of a growth mindset and create valuable shifts in attitudes to learning.

When beginning to use affirmations in your classroom it might be helpful to scaffold the children's responses by co-creating some statements and allowing the children to choose from them. They could be displayed on an 'Affirmations of the week' board and could focus on a mixture of learning behaviours and attitudes such as 'I am focussed', 'I am excited to learn', 'I am resourceful', 'I am helpful' or 'I am kind'.

Teaching tip

As with other ideas in this book, it always helps to model the use of affirmations. Demonstrate the thought processes of choosing one of the affirmations and where possible, explain to the children why you've chosen it and when you refer back to it.

Taking it further

Building in affirmations across your teaching day promotes positive self-esteem and resilience. During tricky learning experiences, reminders to return to affirmations can be grounding for learners. In some classes, it might help to have an affirmation buddy who can remember their own and a peer's affirmation so they can encourage each other when needed.

My jigsaw

'Being vulnerable with the children about my own strengths and challenges opened up rich discussion and willingness to participate.'
Resource and Guidance Teacher – Ontario, Canada

Encouraging learners to understand that everyone has strengths and areas for development is a simple and effective way of promoting self-esteem. This idea can be adapted using the jigsaw template (available from the online resources) for emergent and independent writers.

Teaching tip

Some questions like these might help to guide your initial discussion about jigsaws: 'What happens if one piece is removed or missing?', 'How do we know it is complete?' and 'Is any one part of the jigsaw more important than another?'.

Taking it further

If you're working on building positive relationships with parents/carers to support pupils' self-esteem, you could include some pieces of the jigsaw to be completed as a home learning task. This is a great way to engage parents/carers in self-esteem discussions and to involve them in identifying ways to celebrate and develop their children's strengths.

A great way to begin this activity is to allow children some time to explore jigsaws without any adult-led discussion. Older learners could take on a whole class challenge of sorting out multiple jigsaws which have been mixed up, while younger learners could have a range of simple jigsaws to do independently. Then, begin a 'What did you notice?' conversation. Encourage the children to understand that each finished jigsaw (a full, beautiful image) is comprised of multiple small parts and that each of those small parts make up an important part of the image (much like our strengths and challenges are part of us as whole people).

Introduce the 'my jigsaw' template to the children and, as you reflect on each of the puzzle piece prompts, model how you would complete your own jigsaw. This is a great opportunity to show how you'd approach trickier puzzle piece prompts. For example, when you complete 'I'm really good at... .', discuss with the children how you could get support to fill that piece in if you found it hard to do alone (ask a friend for help, reflect on the last week in school etc). Encourage the children to pay particular attention to the fact that the jigsaw contains multiple pieces and everyone's jigsaw identifies strengths, challenges and areas for development.

Identity insights

'The children were very interested in learning the origin of their name. Discussions were thought-provoking. Everyone shared and felt a sense of belonging.'
Resource and Guidance Teacher – Ontario, Canada

A sense of belonging and positive relationships in a learning environment can support children's self-esteem in learning and beyond. Encouraging children to gain insights into their identity and sharing the information with peers is a simple way to celebrate diversity in your classroom. This idea works best with Key Stage 2 children.

Give each child a folded A4 card on which to design a name label at the start of term. Encourage children to research their first name's origin and meaning. This could be extended as a home learning task to encourage children to discuss the topic with parents/carers. Be mindful of children who may not live with their birth parents and ensure this task focusses on simple online research into a first name's generic meaning rather than why the child was given a particular name.

Encourage children to share the meaning of their name with their peers and reflect together. Explore the connection between names and identity in a class discussion using questions like: 'Do you like your name?', 'What does it mean?', 'Do you think this relates to your identity?', 'Do you have a nickname?' and 'If you could change your name, what would it be?'.

On the back of their name cards, encourage children to develop an acrostic poem with their name or nickname. This can be a great way to learn how children see themselves and can be an insightful, safe sharing opportunity at the beginning of a school year.

Taking it further

After the class have spent time getting to know each other, a lovely way to extend this idea is to invite identity insights from peers. This works by encouraging children to notice something positive about their peers and then allowing time for them to add adjectives to the inside of their peers' name cards. Depending on the group and their relationships, this might require some structured directions (for example, give each child three peers' names to add to so that everyone gets some additional identity insights or provide everyone with sticky notes to avoid any unwanted insights being added). Children tend to be excited to return to their name cards and discover how others see them.

My body, my mind

'The students benefited from teacher-directed questioning focussing on what bodies can do and achieve and less on what bodies look like. Posting the writing frame in the classroom was a visual reminder for the students, especially those who struggle with positive body self-talk.'

Resource and Guidance Teacher – Ontario, Canada

This idea fits well into broader Personal, Social, Health and Economic Education and Relationships and Sex Education work on body image, online influences and the impact of social media on self-esteem. It would be well-placed after children have had the opportunity to discuss that all bodies are different and all bodies are brilliant!

Teaching tip

Some children will benefit from repeating this activity individually using a personalised A4 body shape template (an initial template is available from the online resources). It can be a helpful assessment opportunity to initially let children complete this independently and observe carefully how able children feel to articulate thoughts and positive perceptions about their bodies. With close teacher observation and questioning, this idea could be an informative baseline task before a unit of learning on body image and social media influences.

Begin by inviting an adult to be drawn around by the children; they should lie on the floor on a large piece of paper. Add the title 'I respect my body because...'.

Work together as a class to annotate the body shape with examples of *what* each body part can do and *why* it should be respected. Encourage children to think about their own body's capabilities in this discussion and add as many ideas as possible to the writing frame.

Explain that you want children to look beyond the physical; it's not about *how* a person looks but *what* their body can do and *why* it should be respected. It's important that a culture of respect and care underpins this activity; from experience, I'd suggest doing it once you know your class well as it relies on guiding pupil discussions and potentially supporting children to challenge negative self-concept around their bodies. Some children will need more help to articulate positive self-talk about their bodies than others.

Ten things I know about me

'Keeping the list in a special "warm fuzzy" booklet was wonderful to add to and revisit as needed.'
Resource and Guidance Teacher – Ontario, Canada

Self-awareness and a positive sense of self are key to ensuring a strong foundation in emotional wellbeing. This simple idea can be used to focus children's reflections on what they know about themselves and can provide teachers with an insight into each child's self-concept and how this may change over time.

Introduce the idea of knowing about ourselves and being able to articulate what we know in a class discussion or circle time. With younger children, their initial statements may be predominantly concrete, for example 'I know I am a brother' and, with careful questioning and modelling, they can develop into more abstract 'I know I am loved' or 'I know I am a good friend'. Some children may benefit from reasoning questions such as 'How do you know?' or 'What makes you think this?' to extend their learning.

If possible, keeping the lists and revisiting or editing them or repeating the task over time can be an interesting experience for learners. There's a great opportunity for identifying growth and personal development when reflection time is dedicated to updating lists and noticing increased self-awareness.

Teaching tip

Once initial ideas have been shared, there are lots of ways this idea can be used to promote thinking and writing. As a quick brain break, children can be asked to speed-write their list of ten things with a timer countdown. Alternatively, an end of week reflection task could allow children to think more deeply about what they know about themselves in connection to the completed week of learning.

Thriving not surviving

Part 7

Bubble breathing

'This is a fun and practical way for our youngest learners to practise mindful breathing. Sometimes holding their breath gets tricky because they find themselves having so much fun they start to laugh! It's definitely helped with focus and self-regulation.'
Head of Early Years – Hong Kong

Many schools encourage children to develop awareness of their breath and to use breathwork as a tool for wellbeing. This is a fun approach to meditation which helps to cultivate awareness and focus on the power of breath.

You will need bubble mixture and a large bubble wand. This is a fun idea to introduce during the summer term and to begin using outdoors. Firstly, ask children to sit in a circle and observe bubbles as you blow them. Use questions like 'What can you see?', 'What do you notice about the size of the bubbles?' and 'How long do they float before they pop?' to encourage children to pay close attention to the bubbles.

Next, introduce the power of a slow, deep breath and how breathing mindfully feels. Practise breathing consciously and moving mindfully; you could ask children to begin low to the ground and stand tall as they breathe in, then curl up again as they exhale. Some children will enjoy working in pairs or trios for this part of the activity so they can observe both their own and others' breathing.

Finally, combine the bubble blowing with mindful breathing. Encourage the children to inhale deeply as you blow a bubble and then follow it with their eyes. They should hold their breath and then exhale only when the bubble pops. The larger the bubble wand, the longer the bubbles will last, so this really challenges children's awareness and focus alongside their conscious breathing.

Bonus idea ★

You could also facilitate child-led bubble breathing by leaving bubble mixture and wands in the outdoor play area or by grouping children into pairs or trios to observe and practise bubble breathing with their peers.

Mindful moments

'Mindful moments helps us all to keep noticing the happiest times in our learning environment. Children have become really good at justifying their votes!'
Year 2 Teacher – Dubai, UAE

Being aware of and celebrating mindful moments in our classrooms can help to cultivate healthy habits and builds up a useful bank of strategies. This idea needs an empty jar, scrap paper, a few minutes at the end of every week and some democratic discussion!

Begin by introducing the mindful moments jar to the children; they could draw themselves or something cheerful to decorate the jar so that they begin to feel ownership of it. Choose somewhere prominent for the jar and refer to it regularly.

Next, discuss with the children what a mindful moment looks like; this can be a positive time during learning where all children are engaged and enjoying their tasks, a moment of joy and laughter during a class discussion or perhaps a particular event or exciting occasion.

As the week nears its end, reflect on the mindful moments. This is an important element as it requires some democratic group negotiation. Ask children to discuss and decide which mindful moments they thought were the best that week. You could encourage a couple of children to justify their reasons. Then ask the class to vote for their favourite moment to add to the mindful moments jar. This works well if all children close their eyes when voting so that peer pressure doesn't skew results. Once a winning moment is identified, choose a child to write it on a piece of paper, date it and add it to the jar. At the end of a term, children will enjoy emptying the mindful moments jar and remembering what they voted for.

Teaching tip

Some classes will benefit from listing the mindful moments on a corner of your board throughout the week; this encourages children not only to notice (and suggest adding) mindful moments as they occur but also serves as an *aide mémoire* at the end of the week.

Bonus idea ★

If you want to test class negotiation skills, consider changing the format from individual to a table group vote; this will require children to reason, reflect and convince one another of their choices.

Sparking joy

'We all enjoy sharing and borrowing ideas of how to spark joy in Year 4'.
Year 4 Teacher – London, UK

This idea for a short pause mid-lesson or mid-school day is a fun, noisy and creative way to share positivity within your class. Children are challenged to think about and share something which sparks joy for them – in my experience, this often results in lots of laughter!

Taking it further

As your children begin to develop their emotional literacy, you could stretch and challenge them by changing the emotion from joy to another emotion like excitement or hopefulness midway through this activity. This will mean they have to think at speed and reflect quickly.

You could structure this idea in lots of different ways but essentially, each child needs to come up with something they've seen, done, watched, experienced or heard that has sparked joy for them. They need to understand what joy feels like so it might be worth introducing it as a new feeling through the use of a picture book or reflection on a film extract or music. In order to elicit a range of different ideas, it's helpful to model this to the children. You could consider doing a version of word tennis (**Idea 32**) with another adult in the room, sharing lots of examples of moments that spark joy with the children.

As this is designed to be both a reflective sharing idea and also an active break from learning, encourage children to get up on their feet. I have used a bean bag or soft ball and encouraged children to throw it between them, sitting down when they've shared an idea which sparks joy. They should continue until all children have shared. The challenge can be increased by setting a time goal – how quickly can we share 30 things which spark joy for us? Some children might prefer a table group opportunity to share their thoughts. Each group could create their own (timed) brainstorm of examples and tables could race against each other to keep the pace and energy up!

Cup of calm

'The children love the visual of the cup. It's been lovely hearing about how they find calm.'
Assistant Headteacher – Sheffield, UK

Creating opportunities to help children reflect on and develop ways to cultivate calm can be empowering and impactful. This idea provides a visual context and an opportunity for children to notice how they can regulate their own wellbeing through engagement with other people, places or activities.

The cup of calm idea is a simple way to get children to think about elements of nature, experiences and other living beings which help them to find a sense of calm. Using the simple template (available from the online resources), begin by leading the children through a discussion about things you do to help you feel calm. This could be an open class discussion or you might find it useful to show images or share objects with the children. It can also help the children to visualise the places/objects you mention if they close their eyes and listen to you describe them. Try to include a range of settings, people or activities which help you feel calm and encourage the children to think about how being in nature could contribute to this feeling. Next, encourage children to work in pairs to discuss and document people, activities or environments which help them to feel calm.

Finally, create a classroom cup of calm. Using the template, invite the children to contribute to a whole class collage. You could encourage children to use the internet to search for specific images of places they've been where they've felt calm or to bring in photographs from home of significant people who help their wellbeing. Display the cup somewhere visible for the children and add to it throughout the academic year.

Taking it further

Designing a personalised cup of calm for some children will be helpful to promote self-regulation. In a 1:1 intervention, the focus should be on the child knowing and reflecting on who and what helps their wellbeing and then also being able to access the ideas they've identified as a strategy for self-regulation.

Where will your pencil go?

'We found that praising children's creative responses really helped their engagement with this idea.'
Year 3 Teacher – London, UK

This idea combines key themes related to wellbeing: creativity, process and awareness. It's super simple and can be used as a pause from learning, a calming task to settle after break time or an ongoing opportunity for individual creativity.

Taking it further

Some might enjoy additional challenges such as keeping their pencil connected to the paper throughout. Once children have completed their images, you could suggest they colour mindfully. This can make a lovely display which celebrates individuality and creativity.

Each child needs a piece of paper and a pencil. They can choose to work in portrait or landscape and just need to ensure their pencil is sharp.

Introduce the importance of thinking creatively, focussing on the process and working independently. There is no 'right' outcome and it's important to celebrate the diversity of responses from each child. Once everyone has their resources set up, choose a simple shape or line and draw it on your whiteboard. All children should then replicate the shape or line in the same place on their page. Try and keep the shape or line relatively small so that most of the paper is free for children to express themselves.

Next, let their pencil take them on an adventure. Choose a time frame for the pencil adventure and consider if calming music would help children to focus. Then it's over to them to start at the shape you've allocated and draw whatever they'd like. Some children will keep their image abstract and be more focussed on the movement and feeling of the pencil. Others might create something they've seen.

Once they've had long enough (I've often had to extend the time because they're so focussed!) invite them to take part in a walking gallery (**Idea 85**). This is a great opportunity for them to look at and appreciate each other's creations.

Noticing the small things

'This activity really helps children with their focus and attention to detail. It can be spontaneously implemented within the classroom, during any period of the day, especially if the class is unfocussed. It's been particularly helpful with the impact of COVID and missed socialisation opportunities.'
Year 3 Class Teacher – London, UK

This idea involves children working in pairs, honing their observational skills and having fun. It can be adapted easily to make sure it's challenging (but not impossible!) and engaging for learners of any age. It can also be done as a table-top task in class or in an outdoor learning environment.

To begin, pair children up and have them sit opposite each other. Allocate one child in each pair the role of the observer and give them the task of looking carefully at their partner for a specific period of time (start with a minute; it's longer than you might think!). After the observation period ends, ask the child to write down or tell their partner as many things as they noticed as possible. It always amazes me the detail that some children spot in this warm up! Swap so that each child gets to be the observer.

Next, children choose an agreed number of objects from the classroom to arrange on their desks. The observer watches carefully and then has another block of time to memorise as much as they can about the objects. After the time block ends, the child who has arranged the objects removes one (or more) while their partner observer has their eyes closed. The challenge is for the observer to spot what's disappeared through noticing the small things. Swap again so everyone gets a chance to observe and try to hone their noticing skills.

Teaching tip

Depending on the relationships children in your class have with each other, it might be important to reinforce the expectation of kindness when making close observations of each other.

Bonus idea ★

After children have had an opportunity to notice the small things in pairs, they could team up with another pair. This often develops a positive competitive spirit between pairs.

Safety superheroes

'This activity is great for giving children autonomy in shaping their learning environment and it gives an opportunity to have an in-depth dialogue with the children about different safety needs, and how these can be met through the varying "superheroes".'
Year 3 Teacher – London, UK

This idea encourages children to work in groups to identify a safety focus they could take responsibility for in their classrooms. It can be a good context for discussion about how feeling safe can benefit our wellbeing.

Begin by grouping children and ask them the question 'What helps you to feel safe in school?'. This should elicit initial understanding of themes related to safety and might include responses related to safety in the environment, feeling emotionally secure and knowing it's OK to make mistakes in learning. Then repeat the discussion but this time focus on home and life beyond school. Ensure you support children who may have particular challenges answering this question.

Next, decide as a class which safety superheroes they'll be designing. Some ideas could include a trip hazard superhero who checks the pathways for children to move around the classroom; an equipment superhero who monitors that all classroom resources are stored safely and securely; a growth mindset superhero who reminds all learners that mistakes are a good thing; or a kind words superhero who reminds all learners about the impact of language on wellbeing. Once each group has responsibility for a superhero, they can begin designing their character collaboratively; they may wish to label the hero with specific skills and a name. To conclude this activity, each group can present their safety superhero to the class for feedback.

Bonus idea ★

The drawing of each safety superhero could be framed and then used as a classroom responsibility indicator. Each week, choose a different child to take on the role of each safety superhero and place the relevant photo frame on their desk as a reminder of their role.

Body talk

'This activity is accessible for all students to communicate and express their feelings when verbal communication is too confronting.'
Primary Music Specialist – Melbourne, Australia

This idea builds upon the idea of body scanning where children are encouraged to lie still and focus their awareness on different parts of the body. While cultivating awareness can be very helpful for some children, body talk challenges children to think carefully about how their body might communicate particular needs or emotions.

Bear in mind that this idea requires children to feel safe and comfortable to lie on the floor in their classroom and close their eyes. You may need to make adjustments for some children such as recommending that they focus on a spot on the ceiling rather than close their eyes or allow them to sit in a chair if they would rather. This is an idea best kept for later in the year when you've built effective relationships with the children and know their individual needs.

Once children are comfortable in the environment, introduce the idea of noticing where feelings or emotions are communicated through our bodies. Some children will find it difficult to associate the physical connection if they're not having a specific emotional response at the point when you try this idea; to support them, consider creating a short scenario or descriptive passage which might encourage children to connect to the emotion. Ask the children questions such as 'If you felt nervous, where might you notice this in your body?' or 'The last time you felt cross, could you feel that in your body somewhere?'. Children can then indicate their responses by moving their hands to the relevant body part.

> **Bonus idea** ★
>
> This is a good idea to try with more than one adult in the room. It can be a useful observation exercise, particularly for children who struggle to self-regulate their anger or upset. If an adult can observe and remember where the child identified body talk, this knowledge can be used as a tool in future self-regulation conversations.

My relationships triangle

'This has become a really valuable way to help our children to reflect on what helps or challenges them in their learning. It has been interesting to observe how discussions have then fed into independent work and helped children to become more resilient.'
Inclusion Lead – Oxfordshire, UK

This idea works well with older children, particularly those facing transitions to new educational settings or developing as resilient learners. I tried it after studying work by Janet Tod and Simon Ellis, which highlights the importance of classroom relationships and their impact on behaviour. The aim is to impact the three key relationships – with self, with others in the learning environment and with the curriculum.

Teaching tip

Allow each group to rotate and add ideas to the other triangle points. By the end of this activity, you should have developed a whole class review of how to cultivate, nurture and maintain good relationships with self, others and the curriculum.

Begin in an open space (the playground is ideal) and challenge the children to create an equilateral triangle. Try to avoid giving any feedback at this stage, just observe the children carefully. Next ask them to form three points on an equilateral triangle. If needs be, target specific children who might need additional guidance. If you have another adult with you, they could facilitate while you observe.

Praise positive relationship behaviours you notice. Feedback could include comments like 'I noticed you were confident to suggest an idea', 'I noticed you made sure nobody was left out' or 'I heard you use knowledge from your maths lesson'. You're already modelling the importance of relationships with self, others and the curriculum. This is important context creation!

Once the children are in three roughly equal groups, provide each group with one of three titles written on a whiteboard – 'My relationship with myself', 'My relationships with others' and 'My relationship with the curriculum'. Allow thinking and talking time and ask, 'What might this mean?', 'Can you think of an example?' and 'When might this relationship get tricky?' to deepen the discussions.

When children have had a chance to express their thoughts, document ideas. You'll need a large sheet of paper and a marker pen for each group, with a scribe nominated. Each group should share thoughts on how they can build positive relationships within their allocated theme.

Those at the 'self' point of the triangle should focus on strategies to develop self-esteem, resilience and positivity; they should focus on experiences they've had or observations of how this can happen. This might include classroom examples such as remembering a time when they felt successful or persevered with a tricky task. They may also have ideas from beyond the classroom. Encourage the children to notice the diversity of their strengths.

The children at the 'relationship with others' point should discuss and document ideas for forming and maintaining positive peer relationships and how to overcome conflict. There are opportunities here to refer back to learning in PSHEE lessons. Some children might need support to reflect on friendship breakdowns and how conflicts were resolved. Other children may refer to how they have developed relationships with parents or carers. As always, facilitators should be vigilant for safeguarding concerns and be present to support any child who may need adaptations to the task.

Finally, the children who are grouped together at the 'relationship with the curriculum' point of the triangle should discuss ways to engage with challenges in the curriculum, strategies and resources available for specific lessons and approaches which have worked previously.

Bonus idea ★

Use the relationships triangle for your own reflection on pupils' engagement and motivation. If a child is struggling to participate, there might be one (or more) of the three relationships which need particular attention and support.

Hope target board

'This worked really well with our older children and helped them reflect positively on their place within multiple communities. It also helped our teachers understand more about the communities and groups which are important to their learners.'
Assistant Headteacher – Dubai, UAE

This idea was inspired by the work of Urie Bronfenbrenner, a Russian-born American psychologist who believed a child's development is informed by relationships and their surrounding environments. His themes are greatly simplified here to make this idea appropriate for children but the model (a system of concentric circles which resembles a dartboard) remains relevant.

Teaching tip

Revisiting or discussing the SDGs alongside this idea can help children feel excited and empowered by their capacity to impact change. Be ready to support children who struggle to recognise the communities they're part of or who may have experienced adverse experiences within particular communities. This idea requires great teacher/pupil relationships and sensitivity.

Introduce a large version of the hope target board (available from the online resources) to the children and ask them to think about what each of the different rings on the board might represent. Introduce the idea that, as individuals, we are all part of various communities. This will be quite a big concept for some children so preparing your own model target board can be very helpful (and a positive reflective task for your own wellbeing too!). To do this, put your own name/a picture of you in the centre circle and consider the communities you belong to; you might label the other rings 'family and friends', 'school and work', 'my local community' and 'the wider world'.

Give the children discussion time to reflect on the communities they are part of. These will include their own class, their family and perhaps a sports club, religious group or other community organisation. They should include a global community in the outer ring and this will be a good opportunity to revisit any global citizenship or Sustainable Development Goals (SDGs) work. They can be encouraged to look at each other's target boards and notice similarities and differences. Discussions should be underpinned by a commitment to developing a shared understanding and showing respect.

Once children have labelled each part of their board, introduce the theme of hope. Begin by discussing whether they can put their word into a sentence to assess their understanding of its meaning. Perhaps encourage children to reflect on a time when they felt hopeful. Share some ideas of things which you are currently hoping might happen, for example 'I hope that we will continue to look after our classroom', 'I hope that everyone will show kindness during playtime' or 'I hope that everyone will try their best in today's task'. Through discussion, modelling and using images or word banks as a scaffold, each child should discuss with a partner something that they hope for each community ring.

Perhaps begin by modelling your thought process about the school community. This can be particularly helpful and promote recognition of both similarities in community involvement and differences in hopes among the children. Statements to add to the school community ring could include things like 'I hope that our school library continues to grow so that children can enjoy reading', 'I hope we get to do more buddy schemes in the playground' or 'I hope we can keep hitting our house points target'. Once the children are happy they have chosen a hope for the school community, they can add it to the appropriate ring of their target board.

They should continue to repeat this process until they have discussed and written a hope for each of the communities they are part of.

If you have been working with the United Nations Convention on the Rights of the Child or the Sustainable Development Goals, the children could make links to these in their hope statements.

> **Bonus idea** ★
>
> The hope target boards can include personal reflections about community groups for each child. Rather than displaying them, it might be helpful to store them somewhere for the children to reflect on privately. Alternatively, you could adapt this idea to create a giant hope target board populated with hope statements from everyone in the class.

Becoming environmental change agents

Part 8

Creativity in nature

'Children noticed and used things they simply would not have done without this opportunity.'
Year 3 Teacher – London, UK

Getting out into nature can help physical and emotional wellbeing. This idea encourages children to use natural resources and express themselves creatively. Children can work individually or in pairs and should be given as much freedom as possible!

Taking it further

Encouraging children to reflect on each other's work and to identify the diversity of responses to a shared theme or topic can be a great plenary. A walking gallery (**Idea 85**) can be facilitated and children could be challenged to spot something particularly engaging/interesting/inspiring about each other's responses to the task.

Begin by choosing a theme for your creativity in nature task. It might link well to a topic you're learning about. There are lots of open, wellbeing-related themes you could use as a title for the creative project too, such as hope or calm. Next explain to the children that they'll be creating a representation of the topic using only natural resources. This idea is often popular during autumn as, if your school has an outdoor space, there's likely to be a range of natural materials in varied colours available to your learners.

Depending on the space and resources available and the age/stage of your learners, begin collecting items by completing a nature walk around the school grounds or in a forest school area if you have one. Have a camera ready to document the collection process and be ready to ask children what they think the resources they're gathering might be useful for. Next, set up a space where, for the duration of the lesson their work won't be disturbed - particularly important if your creativity space doubles as a playground! Agree a time frame for creating their representations and set the environmental artists to work. Make sure there's a photograph of each art installation before you move back into your indoor learning environment. These can provide great stimuli for writing or reflection activities.

We're going on a senses hunt!

'The children loved hunting for quiet spaces in school, which really calmed them down in the process.'
Head of Primary Personal, Social, Health and Economic Education – London, UK

Encouraging children to notice their surroundings can help them understand the potential impact of the environment on wellbeing. This simple idea can be used with any age group and can be as short, long, structured or free as your children need!

Begin by reviewing senses and the role each plays in keeping us connected with the world around us. Introduce the idea that noticing can help us to feel calm and practise this in the classroom. Set a timer for 30 seconds and ask the children to close their eyes. Encourage them to listen super carefully and try to notice as many sounds as possible. After 30 seconds, ask children to write down everything they've heard and compare responses. Praise the diversity of responses you'll inevitably receive. Some children's sensory sensitivity makes them acutely aware of sounds around them. If you have time, repeat the task and see how many of each other's sounds they can then hear. Continue this task by focussing on other senses.

Once the children have understood the focus required to tune into their sensory awareness, take the activity outside the classroom and include movement. It can be helpful if all the children are tuned into one particular sense while they're on their hunt. Starting with sound is easiest and can allow children to discover quiet areas in school.

After the children have completed the senses hunt, it is important to spend some time discussing how it felt to focus on a single sense, to tune in to noticing sounds, sights or smells around the setting.

Teaching tip

When concentrating on the sense of sight, it can be helpful to explore the ideas of focus and calm with children. Discuss the benefits of using close observation (for example, in a restricted area – it can be helpful to describe to children that picking an imaginary window can support them in times of worry or stress) as a coping strategy if they are feeling worried or overwhelmed. Ideally, model using this approach with the children.

Taking it further

Connecting some of this senses work with other mindfulness strategies can be a helpful and healthy extension of this idea.

One small change

'The pledge shows children that the responsibility doesn't all lie on their shoulders, but that everybody has a part to play.'
Senior Lecturer in Primary Education – London, UK

While teaching and learning about climate change and our impact on the environment is hugely important, it can be overwhelming for some children. This idea supports children to reflect on the small changes they can make which can have a big impact on their environment.

Teaching tip

There are many opportunities to link the Sustainable Development Goals across the curriculum and using the language of the SDGs will help children to maintain their awareness. The simple ideas listed on the website: www.un.org/sustainabledevelopment/takeaction can be used to stimulate discussions before the children make their individual pledges.

Taking it further

Displaying each child's pledge somewhere visible will help to raise the profile of the school's commitment to sustainability and tackling climate change. Teachers and other adults should include a pledge of their own and model with the children how small contributions can make a big impact.

In a whole school assembly introduce the words local, national and global, and explore what these mean in relation to our capacity to impact climate change. Connections can be made to the Sustainable Development Goals (SDGs) and the work of countries around the world to become more sustainable. Children can be encouraged to identify the ways in which their school has become a more sustainable place to learn and reflect on their role in being active ambassadors.

In individual classes, discuss links between care, empathy and agency to encourage children to reflect on the ways in which they can make changes to their local environment. This can be done easily through an exploration of the local area, celebrating what the children like about it and then thinking about how to care and look after it!

Try linking cross-curricular opportunities such as surveying plants in the playground, monitoring electricity use in classrooms or organising a walking bus to school to minimise air pollution and congestion. Once children have a chance to think about all the ways they could make small changes, choose a specific SDG to lead on as a class and invite each child to make a pledge related to that SDG.

Finding flow

'Seeing children completely immersed in learning is something special. Being with nature and allowing choice meant they were quickly absorbed in their activities.'
Year 3 Teacher – Singapore

Hungarian-American psychologist Mihaly Csikszentmihalyi focussed on developing creativity and experiencing happiness through a state of flow. This idea invites learners to experience a state of flow outdoors – explain this as being focussed and happy in learning. A state of flow can often be cultivated when learners select an active learning task, so choice is key here.

Begin by taking children to a space in your outdoor environment where they will be able to see, hear, smell or touch nature. This might involve sitting on grass, looking at flowers, observing trees or lying on their backs watching clouds. Try bubble breathing (**Idea 61**) or noticing nature (**Idea 76**) as an activity to help children focus on their environment.

Introduce the concept of flow by sharing the definition and asking children when they remember being really focussed in their learning. Share examples of your own. These could include gardening, drawing or anything which allows you to focus and engage uninterrupted.

Finally, children have a chance to move into a flow state by choosing an engaging independent learning task. This could be a jigsaw or mindful colouring. It is important to have a range of flow tasks available and allow the children time to choose.

Allocate around ten minutes for the first flow activity and encourage children to work independently, quietly and with focus. Afterwards, discuss together whether they did feel happy and focussed and if they noticed anything about their approach.

Teaching tip

After the initial finding flow activity, try to spot when children are in a flow state in your classroom and praise this. Be mindful of timing your praise at an appropriate moment (such as the end of a lesson or in an end of day circle time) to avoid interrupting their focus and flow state.

Tree tickles

'A lovely opportunity to connect with nature – the laughter in our playground was a highlight for children and adults alike!'
Learning Support Assistant – Yorkshire, UK

This idea explores the senses and cultivates an appreciation of the outdoors with younger children. Ideally, you need access to trees but this can also work well with fallen leaves in autumn.

Begin by exploring the children's understanding of the connection between physical touch and wellbeing. Ask questions about how they feel when a sibling or friend hugs them or tickles them. Revisit any prior learning about the sense of touch and tell the children they're going to become a tree tickler!

Next, take the children outside and have a look at some of the trees in your playground. Make sure you check first that there's no risk to the children if they touch the trees; your school may have specific risk assessment expectations for learning outdoors. Model the tree tickling task to your class before they have a go.

Look carefully at the tree in front of you, such as its colour and the texture of the bark. Explain you're going to write down or tell a partner your prediction about how the tree will feel when you tickle it. Some children will be able to use adjectives such as 'bumpy', 'rough', 'cold' or 'prickly'. Once the predictions are recorded on a whiteboard or with a friend, it's time to get tickling! Remind the children to be gentle and focus on observing carefully how the tree feels when tree tickling.

After they've had a go at tree tickling (which is often accompanied by giggling!), they can self-assess their predictions.

Taking it further

If you're trying the activity in autumn, it can be fun to apply the prediction, tickling and observation tasks with fallen leaves.

Bonus idea ★

If you're setting up investigative play opportunities in your classroom, children could bring autumnal natural resources to a sensory tray and have access to prediction sheets to use independently.

Noticing nature

'Using natural resources helped our children appreciate and learn from their environment.'
Head of Early Years – Hong Kong

This idea helps children to develop their awareness outdoors and can be adjusted to be more challenging and more child-led.

Begin by talking about noticing with your class. Encourage them to notice using multiple senses and consider making a shared mind map of all the things they notice in the classroom as a warmup. As children will have a range of sensory sensitivities, praise and encourage the diversity of responses you get to the question 'What do you notice?'. Once children have grasped the idea that their senses can help them notice a huge range of exciting things, take them outdoors. Repeat the task and encourage the children to spot differences between what they noticed indoors (perhaps the humming of a projector or the flickering of a light) and what their senses communicate to them outdoors. Revisit the idea that connecting with nature and being outdoors can positively impact our wellbeing.

Explain that the focus for this activity is the sense of sight. Split the class into two teams and set up a hoop on the ground or a tuff spot tray. Half of the class are allocated the role of 'collectors', half become 'observers', standing in a circle around the hoop. Ask ten 'collectors' to bring something interesting and natural; this could be a fallen leaf, conker or a stick. Once returned, arrange the ten items inside the hoop/on the tray and give the children some observation time. Next, ask the observers to turn away from the hoop and remove one object. Challenge the observers to work as a team to notice what has gone missing from the collection. Repeat this task switching roles.

Bonus idea ★

This idea could be adapted with children encouraged to choose objects based on how they feel to touch. Smaller groups of collectors/observers could be grouped together and children could try the activity blindfolded so that the focus is concentrated on the sense of touch.

Energy saving superheroes

'Becoming energy superheroes completely changed the mindset of these children to notice the impact of their actions.'
Year 2 Teacher – London, UK

Assuming a collective responsibility for reducing energy consumption can help children to recognise their potential to impact their environment. This idea provides an opportunity to link awareness in school to action at home.

Start by discussing as a class which ways the children could lead on reducing energy consumption in school; ideas could include switching off lights when they're not needed in classrooms or minimising the number of devices left plugged in over night.

Guide children to also reflect on saving energy at home. Ensure this is approached sensitively and reflects your awareness that some children may be living in poverty or not want to share reflections on their home life widely.

Some children will enjoy the opportunity to design an energy saving superhero. You could encourage children to work in teams to design and pitch a superhero to their peers. Consider how the superhero would be easily identifiable, what their superpower would be and what they'd be called. Once the children have listened to each other's energy saving superhero ideas, they could vote for one to be a mascot for their class.

Next, a team of children should be identified as the energy saving superheroes for the week. Their responsibilities can be outlined in a co-created contract and might include doing a light switch check in the year group's classrooms or designing posters for the school office to display.

Taking it further

Ensuring this idea maintains momentum can be challenging. Raising the profile of the energy saving superheroes can be a great way to keep children aware of their responsibilities and lead to long-term change. A simple way to do this is to let the children design a simple superhero cape or hat to wear while they complete their missions!

Bonus idea ★

All children can be encouraged to take on the superhero role at home. Consider a home learning task which asks children to reflect on the small changes they could make to remind their families to save energy. Some children might like the chance to share how they've led their family to become more aware of energy consumption!

Plastic-free bird feeders

'A welcome chance for learners to take responsibility for nature in our community!'
English as an Additional Language Teacher – Laois, Ireland

This idea requires preparation by an adult, support during the creating stage and a few more resources than the other ideas. Start collecting items in autumn as each child will need a pinecone. If they're not readily available in your school grounds, suggest a home learning task or a mindful nature walk.

As well as a pinecone for each child, you will need lard (or vegetable suet), bird seed and twine or thick wool. Discuss the rationale for making bird feeders with your class. You could contextualise this by observing whether there are birds in your school playground area and ask children to make observations at home as well. The RSPB has great teaching tools for exploring how to help birds in our local environments.

Firstly, encourage all the children to clean their pinecone and carefully tie a 30cm length of twine around the bottom. Next, the messy bit – give each table group of children a bowl with some lard or suet in and challenge them to mix the bird seed in until it all sticks together. Once there is a thick mixture of bird food, each child then pushes the mixture in between the pinecone scales.

To help the pinecone feeders to set, put them in a fridge but if that's not possible in your school, try putting them outside on a picnic table or bench if it's cold enough. The last part of this challenge will need adult support, but it will be fun for the children to watch as the pinecone feeders are hung in a quiet area of the playground. If there isn't a quiet space or wooded area, they could be sent home for children to put in gardens or parks.

> **Bonus idea** ★
>
> Younger children may enjoy the Natural History Museum's idea of making a kebab for birds! This is a great opportunity to develop fine motor skills as children thread cubed blocks of cheese, apples, bread or raisins onto garden wire to hang outside to entice hungry birds.

School space survey

'A great cross-curricular context for learning which engaged our older learners hugely. They have become real activists!'
Deputy Headteacher and Eco Lead – London, UK

This activity helps children in upper-primary classes become more aware of their impact on the environment and collective actions to address the most urgent environmental issues. There are lots of cross-curricular links to science and maths and the results of the school space survey can provide a great context for persuasive writing in English.

On large sheets of paper add the words 'transport', 'waste', 'energy' and 'playground environment'. Put these on tables around the classroom and ask children to suggest questions or topics they could investigate in their school space survey. Encourage them to access age-appropriate sources online to guide their survey design. Helpful ideas are available on the survey resource sheet (see the online resources).

Children should then design a survey for a specific audience; this could involve questions for senior leadership about renewable energy use in school, questions for another class about how much waste they recycle weekly or a whole year group survey about transport used to get to school. Allow time for the survey design and data collection.

Once the school space surveys have been completed, plan an opportunity for the children to share their results with other classes and develop actions from their findings. This could involve presenting at a whole school assembly, designing posters to remind people about conserving energy in school or campaigning through persuasive letters for a bug hotel to be built in the playground to improve biodiversity.

Bonus idea ★

If your school has an eco-council, they may be particularly interested in seeing the results of your pupils' school environmental survey. Where possible (perhaps with some forewarning!), ensure that any contact with senior leaders gets a timely response as this will continue to inspire the young environmental activists in your class.

Spot the similarities

'Love this idea – there's a great opportunity to choose images representative of different nationalities in the class.'
Primary Global Citizenship Author – London, UK

Target 4.7 of the Sustainable Development and Global Citizenship goals highlights the aim of ensuring that, by 2030, learners acquire knowledge and skills needed to promote sustainable development and cultivate a culture of peace and non-violence.

For this idea, you'll need to collect images of your local area (streets, parks, shopping areas, public spaces and religious buildings) and the school environment (classrooms, playgrounds, assembly spaces and dining halls). You'll also need to access photographs or videos of the same settings in other countries.

Children can work in pairs or small groups and it's important to have a whole class discussion before and after. Before introducing the idea of similarities across cultures, encouraging the children to find common points between themselves using a woolly web (**Idea 30**) can be a useful warmup. Commonalities might include physical features, beliefs, strengths or interests.

Introduce the challenge of spot the similarities. Show the children a familiar image of their local environment, for example a photograph of an area by a pond, around a big tree or in a local park. Begin by observing carefully and ask the children to work in pairs to discuss or record all that they notice within the environment in the photograph. Next, introduce a photograph of a corresponding environment from another country. While curious conversations will definitely emerge, try to focus the children on coming up with at least five similarities they see between the two photographs. This may be quite a challenge depending on the settings you use.

Teaching tip

This idea fits well into any global citizenship education as it develops intercultural understanding and diversity. Some sources of engaging images can be found on the spot the similarities resource list (available from the online resources).

Taking it further

An interesting follow-up task or discussion after using this idea builds on language. Introducing and encouraging children to explore their understanding of key concept words related to global citizenship such as empowerment, solidarity, unity, inclusion and respect can prompt really fascinating discussions and be a catalyst for action at local, national or even global levels.

Valuing process over product

Part 9

My learning journey

'My class became inquisitive about the next steps of their journey and using a visual map definitely made them feel more invested in what they were learning.'
Year 4 Teacher – Northampton, UK

Having a positive sense of self can contribute to wellbeing and help children to feel empowered and motivated. This idea promotes self-reflection and is a great way to encourage children to notice their own progress within individual lessons.

Teaching tip

The format of the learning map will probably change depending on the age of learners. I have used a winding road shape with some older groups of children, serving as a reminder that successes aren't always linear! With younger children, a rainbow image can be engaging and some children enjoy designing their own. What's important is that every learning journey has a start point where the lesson begins and an end point where the learning goal is achieved.

Each child will need their own durable learning journey map. There are some format suggestions available from the online resources. In addition to the map, each child needs something to move as they make progress along the journey. Counters work well (although initial them with a marker in case they fall off the map) and I have seen some teachers use a small photo of each child. There are lots of ways for children to personalise the design of their map so that it's something appealing and interesting for them to use.

Introduce the idea of mapping out learning for a particular lesson. Discuss with the children that progress will happen at a different rate for each learner and that each of our learning journeys is unique. When a child is just starting the learning or if they are feeling stuck, they can put their marker near the start point of the map. As the lesson unfolds, they can place their marker somewhere along the map to show how they are working towards the learning goal for the lesson. When a child feels like they have completed the work and reached the learning goal they can place their marker at the end of the map.

Explain that children's maps will be a great tool for reflecting on the process of learning and self-assessing their progress. The aim of using a learning map is for children to understand that they're working towards meeting the learning goal and what is most important is to be honest so the map can be a catalyst for support if needed. For some classes, this will be a teaching point in itself; a safe learning environment is needed if honesty is to be evident in learners' self-assessment.

To get everyone accustomed to using their learning map, make sure that, initially, you refer to them in every lesson. The more frequently children use them, the more they'll get used to the idea of learning as a process, the map as the guide and their counter as a progress indicator. Once children are familiar with their maps, they can begins to use them with less and less teacher direction. When children are clear on the intended outcomes and are working more independently, ask them to place their counter or photo at the start of the journey. Use small pause points in your lesson to ask children to stop, reflect and move their counter/photo along to represent their confidence and how far they're moving in the process towards meeting a learning goal. Asking specific skill- or knowledge-based questions in each lesson will help to guide children. Look out for those who rush to the end of the map; they might need more support in understanding the value of process over product.

Taking it further

Learning journey maps can be used in 1:1 interventions and to support children who may struggle with self-esteem or confidence in their learning. It's important to stress that progress within the process is key.

All about me

'Discussing how the children learn best was a great ice-breaker in September. Allowing them time to identify how, where and with whom they worked best helped a lot. It was also a useful behaviour management resource for any adults covering the class.'
Year 4 Teacher – Northampton, UK

This idea helps children reflect on their own strengths, preferences and needs in learning. It builds on the idea of a one-page profile and can be a valuable resource for adults and children alike. The 'all about me' template (available from the online resources) can be edited for your class. It's important that this is used as a whole class idea as the focus is on recognising and celebrating individuality.

Teaching tip

Once completed, the onus is on the adults to read and refer to the 'all about me' sheets to inform their practice. These could be displayed or kept in an easily accessible file for any adults visiting the class.

Taking it further

It could be useful to share the 'All about me' pages with the children's parents/carers and include a section to focus on home learning. Alternatively, if you're working with a peer mentoring system children may opt to share them with their buddy.

Begin by displaying a range of statements about learning on the board and ask children to indicate whether they 'agree', 'disagree' or 'aren't sure' for each statement. Statements might include: 'I like to learn best in a quiet space' or 'Working in a team feels hard for me'. Start with general statements and adjust them from observations of your specific pupils.

You could capture responses through physical gestures or encourage children to vote with their feet (**Idea 33**) by moving to signs representing the three answers. Once children are used to the idea of responding to statements, introduce questions such as 'How do you know?' or 'Can you think of a time this happened?' to encourage children to justify their responses.

Once children have engaged in the active part of this idea, introduce the 'all about me' sheet and encourage them to respond to the prompts in detail. For some children, it may help to focus on one or two prompts at a time.

A recipe for group work

'This helped children who were reticent in group work as they expressed what they felt was helpful. We added to the recipe throughout the year and it was amazing how ideas developed as they became older and fully understood the value of group work.'
Year 2 Teacher – Abu Dhabi, UAE

This idea highlights the importance of expectations for collaboration. Ensuring all children feel secure, valued and heard in groupwork can impact wellbeing hugely. Co-creating a recipe for group work with a new class gives you something to refer to throughout the academic year.

This idea may work well with concrete representations of recipe books and some pots, pans and kitchen utensils for role play. Older children might respond well to an opportunity to debate and vote for the key ingredients to add to their class recipe after the initial whole class discussion.

In a circle, ask children to remember an enjoyable group task. This could be teamwork in class, the playground or during an extra-curricular activity. Using questioning, elicit from each child *what* worked in their team task and *why* that suggestion should be included in the class recipe. For example, a child might identify that a group work task went well because everyone's ideas were considered and 'letting everyone have a chance to speak' should be added to the recipe.

Whether you role play the adding of each ingredient to a big pot or you encourage children to brainstorm together, make sure that by the end of this activity, there's a written record of the key ingredients for the group work recipe. Once children are in agreement with the recorded points, work together to create a prominent display of the recipe.

Teaching tip

If children struggle to identify the positive behaviours and attitudes in effective group work, they may find it easier to recall moments when things went wrong! This can be a good starting point for exploring the positives.

Taking it further

Consistency is key. Make sure that you refer to the visual representation at the start of each collaborative task. Use the language that the children generated to structure positive praise. If challenges emerge in group work as class dynamics change, consider the recipe as a working wall and make additions where needed.

The noise-o-meter

'By the end of the year, I could turn the dial and my class instantly knew the expectation!'
Year 5 Teacher – Brighton, UK

Helping learners to understand the impact the noise they make has on others is a useful way of ensuring everyone's needs are met.

Teaching tip

It's important to give pupils autonomy over the noise-o-meter. Once you've agreed the language and what each noise level would sound like, make sure that each lesson introduction refers to the noise-o-meter and the optimum level for that task. Negotiation is key; allowing children to feel like they have collective ownership of the noise level promotes responsibility. Building in noise-o-meter discussions to the start of break time helps children see that there are opportunities for them to use 'Level 5' or 'Top Level' voices freely.

Bonus idea ★

Consider assigning noise-o-meter monitors to sound check whether the class is maintaining the noise level expectations and make adjustments where needed.

Introduce the idea that noise can impact feelings and wellbeing. Set up sensory sound circuits, link to science learning and discuss how particular sounds might increase the children's heart rates or could be used to guide slow, calm breathing. There are opportunities to link to learning through music or Personal, Social, Health and Economic Education too; reflecting on genres of music and exploring connections to feelings and sensations in our bodies can be a mindful stage of creating a noise-o-meter.

Once children have experience of exploring sound, begin to work together to decide on the language and the categories for your class noise-o-meter. If the children are part of the design process, they're much more invested in its use! Use a clear display with a maximum of five noise categories. To maximise impact, it's important that children understand not just the *what* (the noise level expected) but also the *why* (it can help them and their peers) and the *how* (they can monitor and be responsible for themselves). The noise-o-meter can be a simple semi-circle shape, split into sections or a ladder from quietest to loudest noise categories. These might include categories such as 'silence', 'inside whispers', 'partner voices', 'presentation voices' or 'playground voices'. A simple template sheet is available from the online resources.

Walking gallery

'We love visiting other groups to magpie their ideas!'
Learning Support Assistant – London, UK

The walking gallery requires no additional resources unless you'd like children to provide feedback for each other on sticky notes or leave counters to vote for peers' work.

The walking gallery is a formative assessment opportunity which gives children the chance to notice the strengths of each other's work and to identify ideas to borrow. Once children have been engaged in an independent task for a short time, use a familiar strategy to signify a pause. Remember that some children will need forewarning that a pause is imminent in order to self-regulate through this transition. Invite children to leave their work on their desk (this could be a story opener in English, a self-portrait or an 'all about me' (**Idea 82**) sheet) and move safely around the classroom to view their peers' work.

Children will often head straight to a friend's table and not all children's work will be looked at. You can solve this by adding structure to the gallery with a rotation (for example, table groups moving clockwise) or specific focus (for example, looking for other people's use of exciting adjectives in a setting description).

Older children could leave feedback for one another on sticky notes highlighting strengths or areas for development. Younger children might enjoy leaving a counter as a vote on their favourite piece of work.

Learners will be excited to return to their own desks to review feedback from peers. It's important to give children time to reflect and consider making improvements based on their peers' feedback.

Teaching tip

Some children will need support on how to frame feedback and to keep it kind. You can build on the discussions from plenary prompts (**Idea 86**) or compliments chain (**Idea 16**).

Taking it further

Once children are used to the behaviour expected during a walking gallery, try extending the space to include multiple classrooms. If you're feeling particularly ambitious, try a whole school gallery block in the timetable; it can lead to busy corridors but also lots of great feedback on learning across the school.

Plenary prompts

'We stuck plenary prompts on desks and children got so used to the language from the sentence starters that it became embedded in their learning.'
Year 5 Teacher – Brighton, UK

Helping children reflect on their learning and promoting metacognitive awareness in primary classrooms can impact confidence and allow children to identify successes in their learning. However, sometimes we ask children to reflect on their learning without much support. This can be difficult for some, particularly at the end of a lesson where their energy has been focussed on the task at hand! Plenary prompts are a simple scaffold to optimise reflective moments in your classroom.

There are many ways to create plenary prompts: some classes use a working wall display where children pick a sentence starter or the teacher chooses one to help them frame their reflections at the end of the lesson. I have found that using lollipop sticks and writing a sentence starter on each works well with all ages. Prompts might include statements such as:

- 'I used resilience when...'
- 'I was most focussed when...'
- 'I can see a connection between today's learning and...'
- 'I need to work on...'
- 'A resource I chose to use today was...'
- 'I'm proud of...'.

To begin with, some children will need support identifying their strengths and it might be helpful to build up a word bank of ways to complete the statements. By guiding the reflective process through teacher questioning and then praising honest assessments, children will get used to the expectation of purposeful reflection at the end of a lesson and plenary prompts can be used increasingly independently.

Bonus idea ★

The plenary prompt sticks can be used initially to target individual learners in a whole class discussion. This allows lots of teacher input to guide and deepen children's reflections. Once familiar with the prompts, try giving each table group a plenary prompt stick to use as a focus for their own independent small group discussion. As they become more confident in reflecting on their learning, some classes might enjoy designing their own plenary prompt statements so it's useful to have a few spare lollipop sticks available!

Small, medium and large goals

'Combining the idea of goal setting with sport was a hook for my intervention group.' *Learning Support Assistant – London, UK*

Identifying targets is common practice in primary schools. Try this idea at the start of an academic year as the children set intentions for the year ahead. Using the small, medium and large football goals template (available from the online resources) will help younger children, while older children could be challenged to construct their own.

Discuss the difference between short-term, medium-term and long-term goals. Agree a time frame for each, for example, short: within the month, medium: over a term and long: within an academic year. It's useful to break the development of each type of goal into separate sessions to avoid overwhelm. Start with the long-term goals.

Show children the football goal template and model that each of the posts and the crossbar of the goal represent a different type of target that children will set. The left-hand post should be something which focusses on academic work, for example, learning times tables or reading a whole book independently. The crossbar should focus on something related to learning behaviour, for example, being resilient, focussed, organised or open-minded. The right-hand post should focus on a non-academic goal. Children can be encouraged to think about a skill related to a hobby such as music or sport. Adults can help children to identify clear and manageable long-term goals for each category.

Repeat the goal design for short and medium-term goals and then either display the goals or store them somewhere accessible.

Teaching tip

Making it explicit to the children that the crossbar (representing a behaviour for learning goal) can impact both the academic goal and the personal goal can be empowering. It is helpful to talk with children about how they can cultivate the positive behaviours for learning they choose. Some children may not be engaged by football so also consider adapting this idea to another sport.

Taking it further

This idea becomes really impactful when children are given regular opportunities to review and celebrate success in relation to each of the goals.

Positivity postcards

'The children are always delighted to receive praise and this has doubled since integrating positivity postcards. Parents also love receiving good news!'
Nursery Teacher – Dubai, UAE

This idea is an easy way to spread positivity about learning and to help communication between learners and adults at home about school successes. This idea comes with an editable postcard template (available from the online resources).

Taking it further

Once the children have understood what a positivity postcard can be awarded for, invite them to nominate each other for one and justify their reasons.

Bonus idea ★

It can be particularly impactful to hand deliver the positivity postcard to the child's parent/carer if they come to collect at home time. Some parents get used to hearing their child's negative behaviours in school so delivering a positivity postcard can be a boost for both the child and their adult.

Before positivity postcards are completed and sent home, they should be introduced to the children, ideally in a whole school assembly. If you're running the positivity postcards as a class or year group, make sure you explore their purpose. Essentially, the postcards are a simple, tangible reminder of successes and they focus on the process rather than the product of a lesson. They are filled in by the teacher and sent home to parents/carers.

Explore how important it is to celebrate our wins; ask children how many of them find it hard to remember what they've done in school. A fun way to introduce the postcards is to note all learners doing something worthy of praise over the course of a week and prepare a postcard for each pupil. Once you've gone through the purpose of the postcards, children will be thrilled to receive one on launch day!

After postcards become a part of your classroom practice, think about how you can maintain their profile and remind children of opportunities to earn one. You could fill out a printed template with the particular learning behaviour you're looking for in a lesson (such as resilience, cooperation or kindness) but leave the name blank. At the end, celebrate the child who has shown that behaviour and add their name to the postcard.

Learning logs

'Such a simple, clear idea. The children felt really important having their own learning logs. I kept one too!'
Year 2 Teacher – Birmingham, UK

This idea builds on a popular three question format for reflective practice which was developed by Rolfe (2001). Learning logs create a valuable opportunity for children to use these simple questions to guide reflections on their learning.

Children will need either a digital document or a paper notebook in which to keep their learning log. It's important to establish good habits when using a reflective journal and this begins by dating each entry. While some children will benefit from a structured point in the school day/week to complete their learning logs, others might want to make additional entries at times of their choice if they find the process useful.

To begin with, model the use of 'What?', 'So what?' and 'Now what?' with the children. Introducing the three questions using traffic lights can help to make clear distinctions between each stage of the reflection in a learning log entry.

- 'What?' in red as a signal to stop and reflect on learning. It should prompt awareness of what has been learned by asking 'What are the key takeaways from that lesson?'.
- 'So what?', in amber, requires the children to make a connection to other learning through questions such as 'What does this link to?' or 'What connections did you make to prior knowledge in this lesson?'.
- 'Now what?', in green, focusses on next steps and can be guided with questions such as 'What do you want to find out now?', 'How might you apply your learning in a different context?' or 'Who can you share your learning with?'.

Teaching tip

Once children are familiar with learning logs, you can use mini-plenaries within lesson time to ask children to stop and reflect. The colour-coded questions could be displayed on the board and children can be given time to reflect. This helps to reinforce the value of reflection on learning as an ongoing, never-ending cycle.

Topic recall framework

'This idea is a great way to develop life skills and reduce anxiety around the inevitable tests children face. Our families also benefit from learning about how children are taught revision skills.'
Year 6 Teacher – Surrey, UK

This idea is designed to support older children with retrieval practice and can be used both during a unit of study and as a revision aid. It focusses on guided reflection to help children access and retrieve knowledge.

Teaching tip

Children should have regular access to their personalised concept organisers; it can be helpful to stick them in the back of a subject-specific book. Alongside individual concept organisers, a large whole class version could be displayed on a working wall. This will help you to use the format and associated language in class discussions and can be a low stakes way to track and reflect on key learning.

Using the adaptable concept organiser on the online resources, introduce the idea of cognitive overload to the children. Explore the importance of chunking learning into parts so that our brains can retrieve relevant information more easily.

Children begin by adding a title to the organiser: for example, a topic title in humanities or a strand of learning in maths. Before the unit begins, children should complete the 'Looking back' box with notes of anything they already know about the topic. This can be a good opportunity for teachers to identify any subject-specific misconceptions. Next, children should complete the 'I wonder' box with anything they're curious about in relation to the topic. This can inform subsequent lessons and support child-led enquiry.

Bonus idea ★

To ensure this idea is accessible for all, some children may need a simplified version of the concept organiser. It's easy to personalise and can be populated with words or drawings and used independently or with adult support.

As the block of learning continues, children should be encouraged to revisit their concept organisers and complete sections such as 'Key terms', 'Connections' and 'New learning'. As the unit comes to an end and a summative assessment is planned, encouraging children to use the resource can help them to see, in a concrete way, just how much they've learned and that the impending test is an opportunity to show what they know!

Collaborating for change

Part 10

Wellbeing wheel

'Our wellbeing lead keeps this high on our radar and we're now used to looking out for ideas and sharing resources with each other on the wheel.'
Year 2 Teacher – Oxfordshire, UK

This is a simple idea which helps encourage all school staff to share resources and can also prompt dialogue. It fits well into a whole school approach to wellbeing and is useful for schools who already have some good practice in place.

In the staffroom, ideally somewhere prominent, create a wellbeing wheel – you might find the display template guide available from the online resources useful. Create sections representing different dimensions of wellbeing, including emotional, physical, cognitive, spiritual, mental and financial. It can help to colour code these sections and you could use the same colours for any other display boards or notices about that dimension around school.

This idea works best if the wheel is started by a wellbeing lead or a member of the Senior Leadership Team. It doesn't take a lot of time but it's important that the wheel isn't left bare for long as this can impact the momentum of people starting conversations. The first person to engage with the wheel can begin to add any resources they're aware of so that their colleagues can access them. This could include information about local religious services, a flyer for an emotional support group, some contact details for a specific organisation such as Education Support, or a discount code for a local restaurant.

Ideally, announce in a meeting that the wellbeing wheel is designed to be a whole staff resource. You could encourage some proactive colleagues to add to it within the first couple of weeks so that it becomes a working wall.

Taking it further

The wellbeing wheel is predominantly designed to focus on staff wellbeing. However, it may evolve into a place where wellbeing resources relevant to parents/carers and families could be added too.

Bonus idea ★

Senior leadership could use the wellbeing wheel as a structure for seeking feedback from teams too; a similar blank format could be shared with year group teams to seek ideas and encourage agency.

Moving meetings

'This is a great opportunity to connect and communicate in a different way!'
Inclusion Lead – Oxfordshire, UK

This simple idea helps to provide an opportunity to promote physical health, to connect with nature and to reset, all while engaging in key professional conversations. You don't need any specific resources, although taking a phone with you so that you can take any notes from your meeting might be a good idea.

If you're a school leader or wellbeing lead who really wants to set an example, why not give your staff the option of moving meetings? When sending calendar invitations or allocating times for performance reviews, support conversations or general catch ups, think about whether any or all parts of the meeting could be held on the move. While sometimes there's a need to input content onto a computer, there are great opportunities to open up significant conversations if you're on the move.

For some schools, leaving the school grounds won't be an option in terms of staffing but even a walk and talk around the playground can shift the energy in a conversation with a colleague. It's important to consider everyone's needs in terms of physical health. Hofstede's work on 'power distance' suggests that communication and culture are interconnected so it's also important to give choices about moving meetings and be flexible in terms of how they're run. Reflection from all who take part is also important; honest questions about how productive a meeting was on the move and whether actions were remembered are key!

Bonus idea ★

This can be a good meeting format for giving feedback to trainee teachers or those in the early stages of their career. Avoiding the intensity of face-to-face reflection on a lesson, particularly a challenging one, can be a supportive way to open up conversations and a practical way to focus on targets.

Team tactics

'This generated very useful conversation with parents, carers and the community.'
Inclusion Lead – Birmingham, UK

This idea focusses on the importance of working as a team to promote and protect pupils' wellbeing. It's a worthwhile idea to try if your school is looking to raise the profile of your work on wellbeing. Similar to curriculum overviews or maps, team tactics are worth sharing at the start of a new academic year or during a 'meet the teacher' session.

A team tactics publication (either digital or in paper) outlines to parents/carers what's on offer in school both in terms of proactive and reactive wellbeing strategies. You could use the wellbeing wheel (**Idea 91**) to format it. From a staff perspective, creating a team tactics publication serves as a great reminder that the onus is not only on class teachers to support learners' wellbeing.

Mentioning as many staff, resources, online platforms or agencies as possible in the publication will help parents, carers and families understand both the complexity and richness of the wellbeing provision in your setting. Remember to highlight key contacts such as the Designated Safeguarding Lead or the SENDCo.

A proactive way to engage parent/carers is also to share some suggestions of how the wellbeing work you'll be doing in school can be supported or consolidated at home. This might include sharing some of the websites in the resource list (available from the online resources).

Teaching tip

Making team tactics publications bespoke to year groups will allow you to identify specific curriculum foci and additional provision such as targeted interventions, after school club opportunities or visiting specialists.

Bonus idea ★

You can use the team tactics publication as an engagement tool if you're trying to involve families more in the wellbeing provision. Perhaps include an offering of wellbeing strategies and events for parents/carers and families and highlight the availability, for example, of foodbanks, uniform swaps or language workshops.

Game changers

'This is a powerful way of reminding staff that small gestures can make a big difference! The more nominations we got for game changers, the more we could see a culture shift in school.'
Special Educational Needs Coordinator – Oxfordshire, UK

It's important to remember the impact that human interaction can have on our resilience and capacity to support children's wellbeing. Sometimes the most informal, brief interaction with a colleague who stops to ask how we really are or brings us a cup of tea at the end of a long day can make a huge difference. The power of connection can never be underestimated in a school where wellbeing is a genuine priority.

Game changers is a simple way of sharing and celebrating our gratitude for simple interactions that make a difference and the ways in which the kindness, knowledge, understanding or patience of a colleague has helped us to thrive. Whether you choose to use a digital pinboard, a wall space in the staffroom or a section of a weekly staff newsletter, what's important is that all colleagues get a chance to contribute nominations. Game changers can be people who are recognised for their specific behaviour for example 'Miss Lindsay is a game changer because she listened to me work through a tricky request from a parent'. They can also be people who spread kindness, are relentlessly supportive or just smile lots even on a dark January morning!

School leaders could invite a weekly nomination from each year group or keep the game changers board as an *ad hoc* opportunity to celebrate great colleagues.

Taking it further

Game changers could also include events, resources or gestures. For example, you could celebrate the impact of the cakes someone left in the staffroom on a busy day or thank a member of the Senior Leadership Team who finished a meeting early so you could get some extra marking finished before school closed.

Policy planning

'This really reminded us how much language and shared understanding matter in schools.'
Head of Early Years – Hong Kong

To promote sustainable change in terms of wellbeing in schools, it's really important that there's a clear vision and understanding of priorities, strengths and areas of development. This idea focusses on ways to embed wellbeing in school policies.

Taking it further

Once staff have worked together on identifying five key wellbeing words which they will then reflect in policies and practice, it's a useful to introduce them to the children. Launching the key wellbeing words through a whole school assembly or a wellbeing theme of the week provides an opportunity to raise the profile of these key commitments across the school.

Consultation with staff is the starting point for this idea. It's important to begin by having an honest and open conversation about where there are strengths in wellbeing practices. What do staff feel is being done well in relation to physical, emotional, cognitive or spiritual wellbeing? How is this evidenced? Next, focus on where things could be done better. Encourage creative and aspirational discussions where teachers and support staff not only identify broad aims and focus areas for development but also consider the resources needed to work towards those aims.

Challenge staff to identify and agree on five key words related to wellbeing which they feel should be reflected consistently within policies and other documents shared within the community. This will be a very context-specific conversation and will need time and space for views to emerge, perspectives to be celebrated and a consensus to be reached. You might find the policy words available from the online resources a useful prompt sheet for discussions.

Often wellbeing words are very closely aligned to the school's values. It's interesting to make these explicit links during the preparatory policy planning work. Small working groups can then focus on a single policy document and review where the key wellbeing words could or should fit into each policy.

Celebratory learning walk

'We invited our Early Career Teachers to join us on celebratory learning walks during their first term. It not only gave them an opportunity to magpie great practice and chat with senior leaders but this shift in focus also took away some nerves about being observed.'
Deputy Headteacher – London, UK

While learning walks are a key quality assurance approach in many schools, they can be quite stressful for some teachers. This idea offers an explicitly positive focus for learning walks and encourages staff agency in the process.

Begin by using some staff meeting time to identify key themes for the upcoming term's celebratory learning walks. It can support a real culture shift if staff are involved in deciding on focus areas. You could try using your school's values or mission statement as the key themes, or the topics identified in Policy planning (**Idea 95**) might be helpful. Once key themes, such as aspiration, adaptation, inclusion, challenge or creativity have been identified, allow staff time to brainstorm ways each might be evident in their classrooms or others. This can be used as a catalyst for the Senior Leadership Team (SLT) to identify good practice and discussions should involve teaching and support staff.

The SLT should announce to staff which key theme they'll be looking to celebrate during each week where celebratory learning walks are scheduled. While some teachers will inevitably still associate nerves with learning walks, the language of celebrating good practice and highlighting positives is easily reinforced before, during and after learning walks. It's useful to also expand the focus beyond the teacher and focus on all adults working in classrooms, the environment and the learners themselves.

Taking it further

Showcasing the celebration of great practice after learning walks is key; staff and pupil motivation can really improve when their efforts and successes are highlighted. This could be done for staff in a meeting or newsletter, or for pupils in a celebration assembly.

You say, we do

'A great way to open up communication between families and school about the shared work being done for wellbeing.'
Deputy Headteacher – London, UK

There's a lot of responsibility placed on senior leaders to ensure they're doing as much as they can, within a pressurised system, to promote and protect the wellbeing of staff. 'You say, we do' is an easy way to publicly document leadership responses to the school community's suggestions.

Taking it further

For some schools, initially displaying the 'You say' speech bubble with a 'Work in progress' sign on the board will remind parents, carers and families of the ongoing work to respond to feedback; it's important not to leave this without a 'We do' tick response for too long though!

Bonus idea ★

Assigning the responsibility for the upkeep of the board to one person can help to keep it update, however, the contribution of you say, we do pairings is everyone's responsibility. All adults in school should be encouraged to share with the Wellbeing Leader or senior leaders when they've directly responded to a request about wellbeing.

For this idea you'll need a display board and some 'You say' speech bubbles and 'We do' tick templates which are available from the online resources. Begin by identifying a display space to showcase the ongoing efforts being made to prioritise wellbeing within the school community, ideally a place which gets lots of passing traffic: a reception area, foyer or pick-up area are good places.

The success of this idea relies on a fundamental commitment from senior leaders and governors to listen and respond to feedback. It's also an opportunity to showcase the diversity of approaches and range of people or organisations who are collaborating towards a shared aim.

When themes emerge through feedback on wellbeing during an academic year (perhaps through parents' association meetings, informal discussions or reviews of whole school SEN support), document them on 'You say' speech bubbles. When you've decided how to respond to the request, add a 'We do' tick template next to the speech bubble. Where possible, include QR codes or links to organisations you're using in school or make a suggestion of how the learning/wellbeing work in school could be extended to home.

Workspace wellbeing guidance

'A simple but powerful way to help teachers protect their time!'
Early Career Teacher – London, UK

Many teachers say that the biggest barriers to their wellbeing are workload and lack of time. This idea can help guide the Senior Leadership Team to explore setting expectations within workspaces which promote colleagues' wellbeing.

Teachers are naturally good communicators; we have to be. Some of us are also inherently social creatures who thrive on adult conversation in brief breaks from the classroom. However, we are also working against the clock to mark books, analyse data, review targets and plan lessons. This makes for a tricky combination in shared staff workspaces in schools.

This idea emerged while mentoring a trainee who was finding they got little done in a shared workspace because they were trying to build professional relationships. While connections with other teachers were invaluable, informal chats or listening into planning discussions meant an increasingly long list of incomplete tasks.

If your school has the luxury of more than one workspace for teachers, consider agreeing as a staff which space is an environment for conversation and collaboration and which is a quiet, focussed working space. This takes pressure off individuals to navigate the social expectations of talking, the need to quietly focus on tasks and the worry about being seen as rude. Those who need to maximise their non-contact time can work in a silent space and those who are looking for discussion can connect without any worry about distracting others.

Bonus idea ★

If space is an issue in your setting, consider how an open conversation in a staff meeting might help some colleagues feel more comfortable. For example, agreeing that if someone is working with headphones in, they shouldn't be disturbed for a chat can be a simple way to ease demands on precious time.

Team triads

'Triads have changed our school professional development culture.'
Deputy Headteacher – London, UK

While many ideas in this book can be supported through informal, organically developed professional relationships, this is a Senior Leadership Team-led initiative to embed sustainable change.

Taking it further

Consider building triad time into the agenda of whole staff meetings. This can be useful for triads to check in with each other, open up conversations about wellbeing and maintain meaningful links. It's also a good idea to think about setting up triads of support staff to ensure this opportunity for professional development extends beyond teachers.

The purpose of team triads is to create an empowering opportunity for teachers to cooperate to improve teaching and learning and also promote and protect their wellbeing. It's important to stress this isn't an additional performance management or quality assurance approach but rather a chance to share good practice, celebrate innovation and nurture a commitment to teacher wellbeing.

To begin with, the Senior Leadership Team (SLT) should group teaching staff into triads. This will require care and ideally reflect a range of experience levels.

Next, a clear set of triad outcomes needs to be presented. Setting a termly triad focus can help this become a manageable and meaningful initiative. For example, starting with a 'have a go' focus for the first half term encourages triads to identify one new strategy or learning resource to implement in their teaching. Time is then made available for two members of the triad to visit the third and observe the new approach in action. Feedback time is essential so it's important to focus on just one theme per term to avoid overload. The second term's focus could be 'ways to wellbeing' and triads can share their strategies for managing workload and promoting wellbeing. Finally, the third term could focus on a collaborative reflection project of the triad's choice, an area of shared interest which has emerged from the scheduled interactions.

Bonus idea ★

If appraisals show clear areas for development, then members of each triad could be matched so that a teacher can see great practice from another in those specific areas. The more diverse the strengths are within each triad, the richer the learning opportunities will be for everyone.

Community wellbeing agreement

'Using our wellbeing agreement in conversations with many different members of the school community has been helpful.'
Wellbeing Lead – London, UK

This idea helps senior leaders to structure key parts of a home-school agreement specifically focussed on wellbeing.

Begin by reflecting on any existing home-school agreements and identify key wellbeing themes (see **Idea 95**). These could include respect, care, kindness, honesty and trust. Assess how the core wellbeing words could be further woven into documents and communications already shared with parents/carers.

Once it's clear that the wellbeing themes are evident, develop a community wellbeing agreement. This raises the profile of wellbeing and puts it at the centre of your school community. Use the five key themes as a structure and create a list of statements under the headings of staff, families and learners. The community wellbeing agreement template available from the online resources can help.

Next it's important to review the draft statements with a small number of stakeholders from each group. Opening dialogue around the five key themes and how they translate into tangible actions for each group of stakeholders is an important foundation to ensure this idea can have lasting impact.

After review and consultation, launch the community wellbeing agreement. Encourage staff to use it as part of parent consultations and refer to it when celebrating good wellbeing practice across the school community.

Taking it further

Sharing your community wellbeing agreement with prospective employees is a great way to demonstrate commitment to wellbeing. Trainee teachers often ask me how they can really tell a school prioritises wellbeing before they begin to work there and a discussion around the agreement as part of an interview could provide a real insight into both the applicant's and the setting's perspectives on wellbeing.

7/261
28-8-24